THE ESSENCE OF
ETHICAL
PRAGMATISM

THE COMMON SENSE PHILOSOPHY

E. Dennis Brod

ISBN: 978-1-4834-5435-1 (sc)
ISBN: 978-1-4834-5436-8 (hc)
ISBN: 978-1-4834-5434-4 (e)

Library of Congress Control Number: 2016910612

Lulu Publishing Services rev. date: 8/29/2016

Ethical pragmatism, the common sense philosophy, is a simple belief based on the assumption that human life has value. It requires the realistic assessment of facts plus analyses and evaluations free of any external corrupting influences in order to determine the action that will produce results in the most practical, or more appropriately stated, pragmatic way.

Contents

Preface

Ethical pragmatism (EP), the subject of this book, is based predominately on common sense. Common sense is a universal quality, and EP is meant for everyone in every culture. EP will help you approach every situation in life, whether it is for yourself alone, or for groups, governments, or organizations of every type.

The improvement that EP affords is based on applying certain standards, including being completely objective and realistic about observing facts, and then using critical thinking without the influence of emotions to find the best way to reach a goal.

As an illustration of one aspect of EP, consider this: If you were choosing a physician to perform a lifesaving task for yourself or a loved one, would you choose a less-qualified physician because the better-qualified one had social or political views not consistent with yours? If you would, in fact, opt for the less-qualified one, you would not, in the opinion of the writer, be exercising common sense and certainly not be following the teachings of EP.

Another aspect of EP is addressed by the following illustration, which although relating to the American culture, can still be appreciated by all.

Let us say that you were thinking of supporting a mainstream political party or its candidate for office in the United States. You would have only two choices—Democrat or Republican. If you then reviewed the respective platforms of the parties and found you favored some values in the Democratic Party but not others and similarly found some beliefs of the Republican Party appealing but others distasteful, what would you do? You would experience the conflict that many of us encounter. If you do choose one party or candidate, you may be frustrated because your ability to remain faithful to some of your values and beliefs found with the other party or candidate will most likely be inhibited.

Similarly, if you feel strongly about one particular issue, there is little opportunity to express your view about the issue without aligning with a particular group, party, or faction. Unfortunately, in most cases, as soon as political parties, persuasions, ideologies, religions, and special interests become involved in an issue, all impartiality seems to be lost. Reason and logic are frequently preempted by name-calling and accusations. The issue becomes secondary.

The two preceding examples about choosing a physician or political party were used only to show how some of your values and beliefs could relate to, and influence, decisions regarding issues or actions. The decisions you make are often imperiled by problems caused by what this book will identify as corrupting emotions.

Although the latter of the preceding illustrations (political activity) involves actions by you that principally affect others—supporting their values and beliefs—much of what we do, like in the first illustration, affects only you or perhaps those close to you. Think of what happens when you are changing jobs, buying or leasing a car, selecting a place to live, choosing a mate, or confronting any other substantial decision in your life. Do you consider all factors objectively, or are you influenced by external factors that are just as harmful as the ideologies, persuasions, and special interests mentioned above? In other words, are the decisions and actions of your own personal life influenced by corrupting emotions as well?

This book is about a philosophy that wants us to return to reason and logic regarding any issue, whether it concerns only ourselves and how we lead our lives, or concerns what others do to affect the entire world. This philosophy, called ethical pragmatism, can help us all meet every challenge more effectively.

What is ethical pragmatism? Well, certainly it is a philosophy. This book tries to explain the rationale of the philosophy in simple terms because ethical pragmatism is really a simple philosophy. As has been stated, its components are based on common sense as well as reason and logic. It also requires accurate and honest assessment of everything under consideration. If you care about getting your facts right and then acting impartially with the goal of getting something to work in the best possible way, you will relate to it.

The concept of pragmatism has been recognized and discussed by philosophers for some time. Although acts of pragmatism have been common throughout human history, they generally have not been part of an organized cognitive discipline. This specific philosophy, which is grounded in pragmatism, has enhancements that render it capable of being formally applied and used deliberately rather than occurring at random. EP is not meant to be simply a subject for study.

One enhancement of EP is the ethical component, which will be discussed in the book. Another component involves using critical thinking, and still another requires ignoring many of the factors that influence decision making in the modern world. This last enhancement distinguishes the philosophy from other philosophies as well as the approaches that are in common use today.

The last enhancement can best be appreciated if you recognize the disturbing phenomenon in our society that is described in the preceding examples. For some time, as is indicated in the above illustrations, it seems that almost always when issues are discussed, the people in the discussion are labeled in accordance with what is stated by them in the discussion. Regardless of the merits of their position, the evaluation of their comments is based on extraneous factors such as who they are or what they have done at other times. What seems more important than their argument is the political party they favor, how they vote, their ideologies, their occupation, their socioeconomic status, their race, their religion, and any other interest they have, whether it be commercial, governmental, artistic, personal, or otherwise.

Today, if one argues in a way often associated with those on the political left, one is frequently labeled a leftist or something like a bleeding-heart liberal. If supporting an argument for those associated with the right, one often is labeled a conservative or something like a reactionary or fascist. It also appears difficult to support conflicting issues in different political parties or among different social or political groups, because many times the practice of not supporting *all* of a group's beliefs is considered disloyal. Thus decisions are often based less on reason than they are on intimidation, a desire to please others, or labels and preconceived opinions. In a sense, this means that we are deciding things based on emotions rather than on intellect. The result of this is that practicality, common sense, and pragmatism as envisioned in this philosophy are all sacrificed.

But how does all this pertain to you, the reader? Well, the seeds of ethical pragmatism were born from the author's experiences starting decades ago—wherein the author witnessed hypocrisy, inefficiency, incompetency, and dishonesty in government, politics, business, and the administration of justice. In many cases the absence of reason and common sense in institutional behavior has impacted our entire culture and filtered down from public expression to all of us privately and individually. It has even distorted the way we view things that are personal to only ourselves. We often form opinions and make decisions that are dictated by those corrupting influences that have become common practice.

Ethical pragmatism wants to remedy these negative practices. It wants us to gather our facts accurately. It wants us to look at every challenge objectively. EP requires that we strip away all references to, and influences by, all those previously mentioned labels, ideologies, and persuasions. We do this so that we can impartially find what works best for ourselves in particular and for humanity in general. This means EP should be used in every walk of life—government, industry, the arts, science, health care, economics, and agriculture—from cancer research to world peace. The philosophy isn't just for lofty undertakings; it is for everyday living in everything we do at home, at work, and at leisure.

Thus this philosophy can do a great deal for you personally in how you lead your life from day to day. And as far as it making a difference in the quest for achieving what works best for humanity, recognize what the author believes about humanity—that there is no more important part of humanity than you.

Introduction

If you can't explain it to a six-year-old, you don't understand it yourself.

—Albert Einstein

This book is about a philosophy that comes alive by using common sense. The book explains the philosophy in terms that make it usable. In philosophical terms, its ethical component is relativist while its main component (pragmatism) may or may not be objectivist, consequentialist, or utilitarian. If you don't care about these philosophical terms, you will probably enjoy this book because they mean absolutely *nothing* in using ethical pragmatism. The purpose of this philosophy is not to induce an academic exercise or provide an interesting subject for an intellectual or social conversation. This philosophy is a call for awareness and action.

A philosophy must do more than attempt to explain. It must do something other than be a topic for a classroom discussion. It can create something or change something, but it must cause something to happen. Ethical pragmatism provides a method of looking at everything in our world in a way that will help us get things to happen. It calls for using our brains and minds the way nature intended them to be used.

Following the philosophy means acknowledging its demands for critical observation of all things in our universe. It compels examination of our goals and how to achieve them. As to existing circumstances, it requires the frequently painful confrontation with the reality of failure. As you read through the chapters, my hope is that the description of the philosophy and ways to apply it will be easy to comprehend and appreciate.

The book is presented in two parts. Part 1 tries to explain the philosophy and give some background and history regarding its development. Part 2 tries to show some ways in which the philosophy can be implemented and may have been used in the past. This is not a philosophy that will provide you with answers to the greatest questions raised by the best minds in history. It is doubtful that any of those answers exist. In many cases the results of laborious study and discussion are worthwhile for improving the mind but do little to guide us in confronting the challenges we face in real life.

Ethical pragmatism seeks to provide a different form of answers than those sought in the abstractions of thought. These answers must be generated by the practitioners of the philosophy themselves in the form of workable actions in the present ... and that means now!

As you will read, the philosophy endeavors to strip away all the labels attributed to people, groups, governments, institutions, and the like. Membership in a political party, the parties themselves, the place where one is considered to belong in the various sociopolitical spectra, religions, beliefs, ethnicity, and so on are of no consequence to the philosophy and should, ideally, be ignored. It would be delightful to be able to eliminate some of the designations used in this book and in making reference to or discussing the philosophy. Necessity compels ascribing some names, because without them it would be impossible to explain or use the philosophy. However, except for identification purposes and to avoid confusion, names have little significance in ethical pragmatism. What something or someone is called bears no relationship to virtue, value, or merit. Once we have applied the ethical requirement that will be discussed later, the focus is totally upon what will achieve the intended goal. Nothing else matters!

There are almost always two obstacles to applying the philosophy. Obstacle one is that not everyone agrees on the desired goal. Obstacle two is that not everyone agrees on the best method of achieving the goal once it is identified. History has borne out that with the necessary determination, both of these obstacles can be overcome with logic, reason, and the constant companion of EP—common sense.

In order to better understand some of the principles discussed in this book, please note these following few points about usage and perspective.

Ethical pragmatism is frequently referred to as EP. A practitioner, follower, or believer in EP may be called an ethical pragmatist, or in a diminutive and easier form, an EPrag.

Although EP is meant to have universal application, the book tends to illustrate EP concepts in terms of the American experience, wherein the concepts are often applied to issues that may be particularly American or Western. Notwithstanding anyone's exposure to, and assimilation of, many cultures around the globe, this is done as a matter of convenience and ease in selecting situations that facilitate communication of the principles espoused in the philosophy. For the same reason, many of the examples used relate to contemporary issues. Nevertheless, the principles illustrated herein are meant to apply to all cultures and peoples everywhere and for all times.

Hereinafter, the word *pragmatism* is used to mean ordinary, simple pragmatism as distinguished from the nineteenth-century school of thought using that word to define its principles. As used herein, "pragmatism" simply means, and "pragmatic" refers to, a reasonable and logical way of doing things. How simple pragmatism and the nineteenth-century version of pragmatism are both distinguished from the philosophy that is the subject of this book is covered in chapter 2.

The book and the philosophy itself urge objectivity. This entails ignoring many influences. It is assumed the reader will be able to distinguish among the influences contemplated by the philosophy and those needed to facilitate order. For example, when the term or concept for "label" or "labels" is invoked, it is not meant to preclude terms used to designate or identify without negative motives—artist, carpenter, nurse, senior citizen, philanthropist, etc. EP ignores only those labels that, in context, are pejorative in nature, such as those meant to suggest a preconceived belief or set of values. This is necessary to avoid, for example, one form of prejudice: the unjustified attribution of the traits of a group to an individual.

Whenever the terms "tolerant" and "tolerance" are used, they are intended to reflect their meanings in the contemporary, social, and humanitarian sense. Their meanings in this context are more akin to a benevolent kind of acceptance. "Tolerance," referred to by some as "toleration," is therefore a kind, fair, objective, and accepting attitude toward and about ideas, opinions, practices, religions, races, ethnic groups, cultures, political persuasions, and ideologies, particularly when there is disagreement. The essence of tolerance is to try to understand others and reach a level of accommodation that allows civilization to function peacefully.

In this work the word *man* in its various forms is used in the sense it was originally meant to be used, as the species *Homo sapiens*. The word *man* does not mean "male" unless the specific context would render any other inference an absurdity. Similarly, the use of *he*, *him*, or *his* and the like should be considered in context.

Herein, the concept of "justice" contextually should include the meaning of "justice" in its broadest sense, encompassing the seeking of improvement of man's lot in any application or endeavor, whether political, scientific, social, or emotional.

"Religion," as used in this book, is meant to include the belief in, or following of, any nonhuman, supreme, or superhuman being or controlling power such as a god or group of gods. All of these are generally associated with an organized system of rules, convictions, and ceremonies that the followers or believers employ for worshipping and applying the religion to their lives.

As used in this book, the meaning of "education" is not confined to one of the conventional, narrow definitions such as its being the acquisition of knowledge resulting from a formal program of teaching. It includes the assimilation of knowledge, skill, and understanding gained from experience and/or any process facilitating the communication of, or reception by the gainer, of such knowledge, skill, or understanding.

"Discrimination" has three meanings according to Merriam Webster: the practice of unfairly treating a person or group of people differently from other people or groups of people; the ability to recognize the difference between things that are of good quality and those that are not; the ability to understand that one thing is different from another. (Currently, the word "discrimination" is in the top 1 percent of searches and is the fifty-first most popular word on *Merriam-Webster.com*.2015). In this book the primary definition is used, meaning that "discrimination" should generally be taken in the negative sense, such as unlawful discrimination or any discrimination not based on a rational, reasonable, justifiable means. It applies to discrimination for reasons of race, religion, creed, ethnic origin, gender, sexual preference, age, limited physical abilities, and other conditions or categories recognized by most civil cultures.

Regarding use of the term "the press," context will normally indicate its meaning. It is generally used in its broadest sense to refer to communication among people and entities of all kinds regarding all human activities. It includes newspapers, periodicals, radio, television, other electronic or nonprint media, news media agencies, reporters, journalists, illustrators, and artists. The concept of "freedom of the press," whether attributed to the US Constitution or worldwide values, contemplates the right to speak, write, publish, and disseminate ideas, opinions, and information limited only by reasonable restrictions to protect others, such as laws concerning libel and the incitement of unlawful violence. Context will also indicate when the terms "the press" and "freedom of the press" are used in an institutional sense or in a noninstitutional sense, such as private communications and social media.

In this book it is necessary to address what is meant by using the word "politics." The word, as it evolved and was adopted as part of our vocabulary, was originally used to refer to all actions of citizens as they relate to any government, power, or authority. Usage further developed to include actions relating to nongovernmental organizations and associations, societies, groups, teams, institutions, and aggregations of people in every facet of life. Today the word "politics" often has a negative connotation, such as in being accused of "politics!" or "playing politics." Many consider the latter usage to be "partisan politics." The book refers to the kind of political activity that we associate with negativity as "competitive politics," indicating a type of political activity that fosters one's own interests rather than those of society in general. This term includes "partisan politics" and extends to all other activities involving self-interest. Generally, when the word "politics" is used, it is meant in the sense of "competitive politics." But once again context may indicate otherwise.

Finally, please note that nothing in this book is intended to take a side, stance, or position on any issue, be it political, social, economic, religious, or moral. Comments on, and suggested solutions to, the various challenges, problems, and concerns in contemporary society are merely illustrations of how EP can be applied in a given set of circumstances. Nothing should be inferred by the reader either from those illustrations or any examples used, since those illustrations or examples may not reflect the author's beliefs or those of any EPrag.

PART 1

The Philosophy

Chapter 1

Some Preliminary Thoughts

Cogito Ergo Cogito.

Many would say that philosophy is a lot of nonsense—and perhaps they are right—but all those who study or teach philosophy should be commended. Anyone who teaches others or devotes any substantial part of his time and efforts to reading, understanding, and appreciating the works of the greatest minds in history is doing something worthwhile. The rest of us cannot be counted among them, because we choose to lead our lives differently. Many of us were fortunate to be peripherally exposed to all those wonderful thoughts and ideas expressed through the ages in various ways. Therefore, it is not surprising that the development of ethical pragmatism was more the result of primary experiences than of theoretical study, although there is still a certain amount of influence from those sources.

No one can identify the first philosopher. Some say it was Thales of Miletus, who lived over 2,500 years ago. Whoever it was, the things he did were not based on what he read from a philosopher, since none preceded him. Nothing written by Thales survived him. Thus the earliest philosophers would have found it rather difficult to find sources enabling them to study philosophy. With almost nothing to study, they did what was left to do. They thought and they discussed. Basically, all of them were thinkers. They thought, developed their thoughts, and tried to express their thoughts. Eventually, when enough of those early thinkers expressed their thoughts—that is, philosophies—in a manner that could be shared with others, we began to have a body of philosophy to study. That body of materials has grown through the ages, and it is studied over and over ... but to what end?

Contemporary philosophy students practice what other students of philosophy and philosophers themselves have done throughout the ages— they seek to comprehend the entire world, often focusing on what is incomprehensible. Ethical pragmatism recognizes the incomprehensibility of so much of our universe while still attempting to find a method of living better; this is done both through understanding those things we are capable of assimilating and making things work as best as we can.

While EP acknowledges the accomplishments of those participating in the various aspects of the academic world, the goal of this philosophy is to avoid the usual academic treatment and attempt to simplify itself so that it could fulfill its very purpose, to promulgate and support what works best for mankind. Metaphysical and other mind-bending exercises, while serving a purpose, do little to help implement a philosophy that is built on practicality. Thus, EP is simple, relatively easy to understand, and capable of being readily implemented. Likewise, this book has been written in such a way as to be comfortably assimilated by all readers. The book is brief, and the substantive content has been chosen so it can be written in very basic and simple terms. In contrast to the usual voluminous philosophical discourses, there are relatively few quotations from, and references to, academic works in this book—such as the one in the next paragraph (for which the writer hopes to be forgiven). These quotations and works were included only because they may be helpful in communicating certain points.

Three of the concepts the book is attempting to communicate—two relating to the essence of ethical pragmatism and the third concerned with the need to avoid being overwhelmed by purely academic jargon and reasoning—are illustrated by a passage translated from the work of Immanuel Kant (*The Critique of Pure Reason*, Preface to the Second Edition, 1787). Many might say this passage is ridiculous, with good reason, but in spite of the form of this paragraph, there is something of value in it once it is dug out. (EP does not endorse this manner of expression.):

> Whether the treatment of that portion of our knowledge which lies within the province of pure reason advances with that undeviating certainty which characterizes the progress of science, we shall be at no loss to determine. If we find those who are engaged in metaphysical pursuits, unable to come to an understanding as to the method which they ought to follow; if we find them, after the most elaborate preparations, invariably brought to a stand before the goal is reached, and compelled to re-trace their steps and strike into fresh paths, we may then feel quite sure that they are far from having attained to the certainty of scientific progress and may rather be said to be merely groping about in the dark. In these circumstances we shall render an important service to reason if we succeed in simply indicating the path along which it must travel, in order to arrive at any results—even if it should be found necessary to abandon many of those aims which, without reflection, have been proposed for its attainment.

Simply reading the foregoing paragraph, selected from an *enormous* body of material, can summarize the three essential points relevant to EP:

1. According to Kant, if something seems to work, you should do it;
2. According to Kant, if it doesn't work, replace it, and
3. According to EP, *there is no need to engage in such extensive verbiage* to arrive at Kant's (and EP's) conclusion.

Thus, the paragraph above suggests what anyone could have independently determined many years ago and what has become a major component of EP. It can be characterized this way: reasoning, talking, speculating, and theorizing are great, but if it looks as though it's going to work, *let's just get it done!* You can always change it later. In this context, it is not necessary to go as far as the brilliant philosopher Ludwig Wittgenstein, when he said that a serious and good philosophical work could be written consisting entirely of jokes. Nor do we need to distill literary aphorisms such as those written by Friedrich Nietzsche. EP does not consist of jokes or aphorisms, but it was designed to be, and is, a working, flexible, evolving, practical philosophy.

In addressing this aspect of EP, once again it is easiest to communicate and comprehend it in the simplest terms. There is an old, respected adage about leaving "well enough alone." This adage was reinterpreted through the years to become the American folk phrase "If it ain't broke, don't fix it." Of course, all such notions must be applied with caution, as there are few opportunities in human existence to be guided by absolutes. Acceptance of this form of modified relativism leads us to the notion that even with what seems to be perfection there is most likely a possibility of improvement. Blending these concepts together, we can reasonably infer that if something is not working, it should be fixed, and if it is working, we should accept it but still seek to improve it.

As you read this book, you will find many references to practicality and objectivity, along with the need for judicious application of compassion. This ostensible inconsistency is not difficult to understand and support once one appreciates the history and evolution of the belief and assimilates the principles of the philosophy of ethical pragmatism.

At this point there should be some explanation as to why the author believes in EP. Regarding the philosophical jargon "Cogito Ergo Cogito" (I think therefore I think) at the beginning of this chapter, no disrespect is meant to Rene Descartes, who concluded, "Cogito Ergo Sum" (I think therefore I am). Descartes was a great—please excuse the pun—*thinker* and contributor to cultural development in Western civilization. "Cogito Ergo Cogito" is really a reflection of a "cognitive" personality, the type describing the author. Many of us, including the author, have struggled to become a cognitive personality at various times in our lives. Eventually, most of us are mature enough at a certain point to adopt a method of dealing with life in a particular manner … whether it is called our own philosophy or something else. The author calls his method a philosophy.

When we are young, it is more difficult for us to separate emotions from intellect in approaching life's challenges. In fact, psychologists tell us that this faculty doesn't really start until we are twelve or thirteen. Even as we approach or attain adulthood and have the ability to so reason, we still have a conflict. Although we may attempt to act according to our intellectual mental processes only, the overriding and constant impact of our emotions always seems to inject itself into the equation. This is particularly difficult with EP because compassion is necessary in implementing the philosophy. Notwithstanding this conflict, if we really want to, we are all capable of using the philosophy without reliance on those "corrupting emotions"—which are rooted in attitudes causing us to view the world in simplistic and primitive ways.

A transition to a more mature manner of thinking, whether through normal maturity or through education or simple revelation, can bring greater insight to, and appreciation of, life itself. It is significant that many of life's corrupting emotions are related to self-aggrandizement. Some are related to insecurities, neuroses, hatred, vengeance, envy, jealousy, bigotry, nepotism, misplaced loyalties, and even the instinct to survive. One emotion that *is* deserving of inclusion in EP is compassion. This emotion embraces the notion that others on this earth have the same intrinsic values as we have. Although the use and application of compassion, like all other actions, must be judicious, it is an emotion that can actually enable pragmatism rather than hinder it (as may be gathered from some examples later on in the book). Compassion is the mother of kindness, and there can never be too much kindness in any human endeavor. So compassion is incorporated in exercises applying EP for its intrinsic worth and because it is consistent with EP's basic premise—that human life has value.

In other than perhaps a purely scientific context, objectivity is not absolute. Whatever thought process is used to apply the philosophy required in EP, discipline is needed to attain a kind of "tempered objectivity" regarding compassion to make a commonsense determination that will nevertheless be consistent with the principles of ethical pragmatism. This tempered objectivity regarding compassion is applied only in the effect phase of an EP exercise; that is, in assessing the outcome or ultimate goal. The other steps require maximum objectivity and impartiality.

While we must apply the sense of ethics and the compassion just addressed, it nevertheless remains imperative that in order to apply the EP philosophy, facts must be gathered from hard, cold, emotionless observations. Success can be achieved only through the recognition of reality. Some would call this approach empiricism, but whatever it is called, the practice remains the same. There is no place in EP for what we now call "leaps of faith." A leap of faith could not appeal to an EPrag. Even something as basic and accepted as Descartes's jump from "I think" to "I am" is merely a hypothetical assumption.

The metaphor of the eight-ounce tumbler containing four ounces of liquid is not a perfect analogy, but it is a useful illustration of the point. It is said that optimists look at the eight-ounce tumbler and conclude that the glass is half-full, while pessimists conclude the glass is half-empty. An EPrag could never be comfortable concluding either. For an EPrag, the glass contains four ounces … not more, not less. It is exactly what it is, not what some extraneous feeling dictates.

In deference to C. Lloyd Morgan, to whom the well-known phrase "trial and error" is attributed, I feel compelled to express an objection. The technique represented by the phrase has been proved to be of great use in every imaginable application. But why trial and "*error*"? Is there an assumption that there will always be an error? Or that there will be more errors than successes? Why not "trial and success" to validate a principle? I have always believed, and an EPrag would concur, that the more appropriate phrase should be "trial and result." There could be a success in the first try and never an error! This is not nitpicking. It is the recognition of a principle that the mind should not make unsupported assumptions. Thus, as in the Cogito Ergo Cogito example above, in almost all analyses, the EPrag will not project "I think" any further than "therefore I think" without some compelling force based on a scientific, practical, and yes, compassionate justification.

The point is that avoiding the leap of faith is not done in order to preclude creative thinking or the contemplation of the next step. The reason not to leap is to allow focusing on the intrinsic reality of what is observed. Without the recognition of reality, any forward action is doomed.

Thus, the paradigms and other creations falling within the scope of ethical pragmatism must reflect reality, or they can have no validity. They cannot form the basis of any plan, project, or undertaking. The omnipresent EP admonition is to beware of euphemisms, hyperbole, ideologies, labels, mendacity, political correctness, and "spin" (in its contemporary usage), because in most cases they are all enemies of reason.

It is hoped that this concept will be made clearer as you read on.

Chapter 2

Some History

The test of real and vigorous thinking, the thinking which ascertains truths instead of dreaming dreams, is successful application to practice.

—John Stuart Mill

Pragmatism is not new. Aside from the many philosophers who have studied it, referred to it, analyzed it, and argued about it, humans have been learning about how to be pragmatic since they first became humans. They did it to stay alive and propagate our race. At some point when pragmatism was absent or when it did not help, some humans died out. The ones who survived may have been sufficiently pragmatic to overcome nature's formidable challenges as well as the aggressive actions of other humans. These survivors became our ancestors.

It is important to note that in terms of ethical pragmatism, or, for that matter, any philosophy rooted in pragmatism, a meaningful discussion does not involve quoting writers and philosophers of the past. In a purely academic setting it may be desirable, even admirable, to spew forth concepts, verbiage—chapter and verse—with impeccably detailed attribution. The contents of this book, however, are not meant to prepare PhD candidates for oral examinations. For EP purposes, one's thoughts and beliefs mean more than all the debate in the world. Finding the best way to act is based on accurate observations, unbiased conclusions, reason, logic, and, most of all, common sense.

Nevertheless, there is value in tracing some of the history contributing to EP as it has been developed. It is also helpful to distinguish EP from other forms of, and theories about, pragmatism. What follows is presented only to give some perspective on what other thinkers may have done and concluded in the past. These following paragraphs have only slight relevance to true ethical pragmatism, but it is interesting to note some common roots as well as differences.

By comparison, here are some definitions/explanations of simple "pragmatism" and its history:

The Oxford Dictionaries, (*OED Online.* February, 2016. *Oxford University Press)* say that pragmatism is an approach assessing the truth of the meaning of theories or beliefs in terms of the success of their practical application, while Merriam-Webster, (*Merriam-Webster.com*.2015*)* defines it as a reasonable and logical way of doing things or thinking about problems that is based on dealing with specific situations rather than on ideas and theories.

In continuing to define pragmatism, Merriam-Webster adds the history of the American movement in philosophy founded by C. S. Peirce and William James in the nineteenth century. That movement was marked by doctrines holding that the meaning of conceptions is to be sought in their practical bearings, that the function of thought is to guide action, and that truth is preeminently to be tested by the practical consequences of belief.

In the popular encyclopedia Wikipedia *(http://en.wikipedia.org/),* contributors recounting the conventionally accepted outlook, describe pragmatism as a philosophical tradition that began in the United States around 1870 rejecting the idea that the function of thought is to describe, represent, or mirror reality. Rather, it is stated, pragmatists develop their philosophy around the idea that the function of thought is as an instrument or tool for prediction, action, and problem solving. Pragmatists, therefore, contend that most philosophical topics—such as the nature of knowledge, language, concepts, meaning, belief, and science—are all best viewed in terms of their practical uses and successes rather than in terms of representative accuracy.

In the same vein, the Wikipedia contributors also describe the origins of the word as being from the Greek *pragma*, a thing, a fact, possibly coming from the word *prassō*, meaning to pass over or achieve. They further define pragmatism as a piece of technical terminology in philosophy referring to a specific set of associated philosophical views originating in the late twentieth century. However, the phrase is often confused with "pragmatism" in the context of politics (which refers to politics or diplomacy based primarily on practical considerations, rather than on ideological notions), and with a nontechnical use of "pragmatism" in ordinary contexts referring to dealing with matters in one's life realistically and in a way that is based on practical rather than abstract considerations.

Dictionary.com (*Pragmatism, Dictionary.com*) stays in the mainstream of definition of pragmatism with references to both the basic definition and the philosophical movement by calling it a character or conduct that emphasizes practicality. It refers to the philosophical *movement* as a system having various forms, but generally stressing practical consequences as constituting the essential criterion in determining meaning, truth, or value.

As would be appropriate, the Internet Encyclopedia of Philosophy (*Pragmatism, Internet Encyclopedia of Philosophy, http://www.iep.utm.edu/, June 9, 2016.*) expresses the philosophical aspects of the word/term/concept as follows:

> Pragmatism is a philosophical movement that includes those who claim that an ideology or proposition is true if it works satisfactorily, that the meaning of a proposition is to be found in the practical consequences of accepting it, and that unpractical ideas are to be rejected. Pragmatism originated in the United States during the latter quarter of the nineteenth century … it has significantly influenced non-philosophers—notably in the

fields of law, education, politics, sociology, psychology, and literary criticism ..."

It goes on to amplify the relatively recent use of the word by recounting the nineteenth-century publications by William James (1842–1910), who seems to have pressed the word into service during an 1898 address entitled, "Philosophical Conceptions and Practical Results," delivered at the University of California, Berkeley. The encyclopedia points out that James, to his credit, scrupulously swore that the term had been coined almost three decades earlier by his compatriot and friend C. S. Peirce (1839–1914). Significantly, as it is further reported, "Peirce, eager to distinguish his doctrines from the views promulgated by James, later relabeled his own position 'pragmaticism'—a name, he said, 'ugly enough to be safe from kidnappers'." The third major figure of classical pragmatists is then mentioned—John Dewey (1859–1952)—after whose death the philosophy seems to have dissipated.

Regarding a previous paragraph's statement about the alleged influence of the late nineteenth-century pragmatism movement on fields other than philosophy, I have my doubts. The people of that era who took those actions most likely did so from an innate belief and understanding about how to attain goals. In all likelihood they didn't care or even know about James or Peirce. James and Peirce were engaged in debating the theory of whether an ideology or proposition is true if it works and other similar theories. The people who just got out there and did everything during that period were part of that great nineteenth-century enthusiasm causing a rise from mediocrity to bringing a great nation to the pinnacle of world success.

Some observers say elements in ethical pragmatism are similar to those in Ayn Rand's philosophy of objectivism. This is probably true, as it is with certain elements of the nineteenth-century and early twentieth-century ideas in this area. The *Ayn Rand Lexicon*, commenting on the likes of Peirce, James, and Dewey, indicates that they held the belief that: (1) philosophy must be practical and that practicality consists of dispensing that with all absolute principles and standards, (2) that there is no such thing as objective reality or permanent truth, (3) that truth is that which works, and its validity can be judged only by its consequences, (4) that no facts can be known with certainty in advance, and anything may be tried by rule of thumb, and (5) that reality is not firm, but fluid and "indeterminate," and "that there is no such thing as a distinction between an external world and a consciousness (between the perceived and the perceiver), there is only an undifferentiated package-deal labeled 'experience,' and whatever one wishes to be true, is true, whatever one wishes to exist, does exist, provided it works or makes one feel better."

The lexicon goes on to describe a later school of more Kantian pragmatists that amended this philosophy as follows:

> If there is no such thing as an objective reality, men's metaphysical choice is whether the selfish, dictatorial whims of an individual or the democratic whims of a collective are to shape that plastic goo which the ignorant call 'reality,' therefore this school decided that objectivity consists of collective subjectivism—that knowledge is to be gained by means of public polls among special elites of 'competent investigators' who can 'predict and control' reality—that whatever people wish to be true, is true, whatever people wish to exist, does exist, and anyone who holds any firm convictions of his own is an arbitrary, mystic dogmatist, since reality is indeterminate and people determine its actual nature.

In spite of what appears in the preceding paragraphs, a philosophy can and should be something concrete and of value in everyday existence. As was indicated at the beginning of this chapter, EP was neither developed nor designed to be a mind-bending super-intellectual exercise. It is for real life in the real world, which is inhabited by real people with real needs, real challenges, and real goals.

There are two major differences between what can be read regarding other ideologies incorporating the word or concept of pragmatism and the subject of this book, the philosophy of ethical pragmatism. They are as follows:

First—That EP is, in fact, pragmatic. All the energy historically expended by scholarly predecessors in their efforts, theories, conclusions, and uses connected with pragmatism were academic. Basically speaking, these individuals were not very pragmatic. EP works now, will continue to work, and, if applied in life situations, will improve the existence of life in our universe.

Second—That there is the addition of a very important modifier, the word *ethical*, to the term for the philosophy.

A third, less significant, but nonetheless interesting difference between what has been related about pragmatism and other pragmatic philosophers and the teachings of EP belongs more in a philosophy class than in this book. These historical philosophers tended to use the outcome (theoretical, of course) of an act to define and validate their pragmatism. In other words, the result determines whether the act is pragmatic. In a classroom, this leads nowhere. EP does not bother to define itself, because it is not relevant to getting something to work or to work better. EP simply evaluates the result without attempting to validate or define the act. If the desired goal is achieved, the exercise is over. If the goal is not achieved or requires modification, another act is sought until there is success.

People, governments, businesses, armies, groups, teams, institutions, and organizations are all continually making pragmatic determinations and decisions upon which they act. We get vaccinated so we don't get the disease. We put money in the parking meter so we don't have to pay a fine. We get to work on time so we don't lose our jobs. These acts by individuals and more complex acts by institutions and others are so common we do not even give the slightest thought as to how they came about. These are acts of "inadvertent pragmatism." To a large measure, acts of inadvertent pragmatism are so routine and without harm that they pose no problem for society. They differ, however, in two very significant ways from EP: First, EP requires analysis and a conscious, deliberate evaluation before an action is taken, and second, these acts have not applied the ethical standard as EP does. On a small scale this may not cause any difficulty, but the trouble begins when governments or any large entities act without the proper observations, analyses, and evaluations necessary to draw the right conclusions (see chapter 7, "Cause and Effect"). This process is a required component of EP, but it is not more important than the imposition of ethics as EP defines them. Whether the process of analysis and evaluation is undertaken, whether the act is inadvertent or not, the ethical standards must be applied.

Inadvertent pragmatism is an unconscious and often automatic action. The true EPrag does not need to convert everyday functions into an exercise in EP. However, in order to practice EP in a manner that addresses challenges that transcend the ordinary, such as those obviously requiring a conscious decision before action is taken, it is necessary to engage in critical thinking. Critical thinking is more than making a technical observation and analysis. It requires the conscious abandonment of all corrupting influences. Politics, religion, and ideologies have no part in this. There are numerous ways to approach any set of circumstances. One particular thought process is described in chapter 7, but any method will suffice if it involves an accurate observation of reality combined with an analysis meant to support action that will produce the desired result.

When we are speaking about consciously applying EP principles, it means applying it to everything—systems, laws, government actions and programs, institutions, the weather, entertainment, health, education, clothing, food, shelter, relationships, and on and on. Anything you can observe with any of your senses is a candidate for improvement, innovation, or some conclusion that will be helpful in leading your life.

The ethical component of pragmatism is mentioned repeatedly for a good reason. "Ethical" may only be a modifier of the core of the philosophy, but it is essential. Pragmatism, in and of itself, can go nowhere but to ruin. It must be tempered by a set of subjective values based on a group of assumptions or hypotheses. In this case, the principal hypothesis is that all human life has value. Just think of pure pragmatism being applied in any number of situations without the ethical component. Do you have competition? Kill your opponents. Do you want to reduce the costs of caring for the sick? Kill all the sick people. These are extreme examples, but societies have done things like these out of expediency and practicality; that is, pragmatism. Thus the ethical component of EP requires that all ends consider, and ultimately employ, only those means that accommodate the basic humanitarian morals and values of our society. This is not an obstacle—it is a noble part of seeking and finding the great goals capable of being achieved by mankind.

Chapter 3

Philosophers Are Only People

We have to dare to be ourselves, however frightening or strange that self may prove to be.

—May Sarton

I cannot teach anybody anything. I can only make them think.

—Socrates

What is a philosopher? There are a number of definitions. One definition is simply someone interested in philosophy. Classicists might say a philosopher is someone who spends his life focusing upon existential questions about the role of humans in our universe. In a 2010 *New York Times* article, philosopher and philosophy professor Simon Critchley likened definitions of "philosopher" to definitions of "philosophy," stating, "There are as many definitions of philosophy as there are philosophers—perhaps there are even more. After three millennia of philosophical activity and disagreement, it is unlikely that we'll reach consensus …"

Some define a philosopher as one pursuing the formal study of philosophy. To me this definition misses the mark. Simply studying the works of others is not enough. This definition could leave out some of the earliest philosophers, who had no philosophy to study. Based on my observations,

I characterize what others seem to believe—that a philosopher is any intellectual, in the broadest sense, who makes a contribution to any of the fields of study that are grounded in philosophy. My definition is perhaps more restrictive. I would say something like this: a philosopher is anyone who (1) conceives of, or develops, a personal perspective on how to lead one's life; (2) organizes the components of the perspective with critical reasoning; (3) defines the body of work as a philosophy; and (4) communicates the philosophy to others in a systematic manner. That definition leaves the field open to almost anyone who cares to develop a belief or way of thinking. It also allows for all different kinds of philosophies, not all of which may be beneficial to mankind. I certainly hope that this philosophy, ethical pragmatism, will be considered to be a contribution for betterment.

Believing that all my thoughts and ideas are original would be most gratifying to my ego, but inasmuch as humans have been producing and memorializing their output for millennia, reality compels acknowledgment that many of the things I think and write may have been thought and written before. There are, however, a number of what I truly believe to be my own perspectives, perceptions, concepts, and word/phrase usages in my works, some of which were derived from the influences of others and some of which germinated independently.

For the purposes of the next few paragraphs, I consider that there are two categories of students—matriculated and autodidactic. Simply stated, the matriculated students learn principally in a structured academic environment, and the autodidacts study autonomously. My view is that a student who is the product of a combination of the two methods of study will enjoy a greatly enhanced learning experience and possibly benefit from a richer education.

Although I was a matriculated student in many subjects and areas of study—including the arts, sciences, and law—I cannot say with conviction that I am a "student" of any the specific fields of philosophy, political science, sociology, psychology, biology, physics, chemistry, etc., although I have had exposure to all of them in varying degrees. To assert that I was such a "student" would be disserving to those who spend so much of their time and labors pursuing expertise in the body and complexities of materials in those fields. What I can say is that I am an autodidact regarding almost everything I can appreciate in my universe. There is no academic degree, no license, no job title, no teaching position, nor anything else officially recognizing this pursuit or status, yet I am proud of having attempted to emulate some of history's greatest thinkers and would be gratified if all those capable would do the same.

At the early stages of my maturity—when I first was exposed to, and fascinated by, the world of philosophers and their quest for all those elusive answers to eternal questions—I actually thought of what it might be like to spend my entire life in an intellectual pursuit studying and searching as did those great thinkers of the past. What would it be like to start as a philosophy major in college and continue that course of study? Would I solve the mysteries of the universe? Would I find the answers to all of life's essential questions? Perhaps I would fail at my quest but ultimately become wise. But what is wisdom? It seems that even defining "wisdom" could be a life's work with no conclusions. This is what the lifelong study of philosophy might entail.

Wisdom is only one of antiquity's four principal, or cardinal, virtues. There are innumerable definitions of wisdom from myriad sources. There are perspectives of wisdom by philosophers, educators, scientists, psychologists, and theologians. Among theologians there are interpretations by the institutions of Christianity, Buddhism, Hinduism, Confucianism, Judaism, Islam, and other religions. There are beliefs in such diverse sources as Mesopotamian and Norse mythologies—and these about wisdom alone! For me, the formula for wisdom is simple; it is a cultural compound consisting of experience and common sense. This is another illustration of what EP attempts to do—simplify the task, and get on with it. It doesn't matter if the task is about the loftiest concept or about something as basic as a definition. This is what works for me, and it can work for everyone. Simple is not simplistic.

But what about the other three virtues—courage, justice, and temperance? Again, the volume of definitions and material relating to these concepts is staggering. Then aside from the four virtues and innumerable other words, terms, and subjects, there are branches of philosophy, such as aesthetics, epistemology, ethics, logic, and metaphysics. In addition to these, there are time periods of philosophy, such as the ancient, medieval, modern, and contemporary. Then there are various philosophical traditions, such as the analytic, Continental, Eastern, Islamic, Platonic, and Scholastic. This goes on and on.

Realization of the enormity of undertaking a life in philosophy was probably the beginning of my disillusionment. Perhaps it was also the beginning of my intellectual maturity. I began to feel that limiting study to even just one small aspect of what was available in the world of philosophy would be an endless, circular struggle—rewarding to many, but hopelessly frustrating to others. I concluded that I would have been one of the frustrated others.

I realized that searching for answers to questions like "What is the meaning of life?" provided a great ride but led to no destination. In fact, it became clear that the most likely result in me from philosophical exercises would be a headache. I did not want to abandon the kind of critical thinking that could be so useful in helping to lead a productive and rewarding life, but I had difficulty in justifying the devotion of that same life to this kind of study. This realization plagued me for a while until my epiphany arrived over one-half century ago. In order to organize my thoughts for an argument favoring the position I was about to take, I wrote a memo that I thought about submitting to my professor. I never submitted it, probably for fear the reaction might have cost me a reduction in my grade, but the thoughts are as valid today as they were then. This is essentially what I thought:

The study of philosophy as a life's work is counterproductive to being a philosopher for several reasons:

1. If begun too early, the student most likely will lack the emotional and intellectual maturity necessary to exercise good judgment

in selecting works to study and, as to those studied, to make meaningful evaluations of them.

2. If studied too intensely, particularly to the exclusion of other studies and activities, the student will most likely be over-influenced by the writings of others, thus precluding the development of the student's own beliefs and theses.

3. If studied too intensely, particularly to the exclusion of other studies and activities, the student will most likely be disadvantaged in lacking the life experiences necessary to appreciate theories, theses, and beliefs in the light of reality.

4. If studied too intensely, particularly to the exclusion of other studies and activities, the student will most likely be caught in a web of theory, doctrine, and vernacular with little regard for actual life and living.

I further thought:

> A twentieth-century student has potential exposure to the teachings and writings of hundreds of philosophers and almost inexhaustible sources of commentary and other texts and literature. How much of this is necessary?

> How much material was available to Plato prior to his writing *The Republic*?

Incidentally, as I reflect on this last comment about Plato, it is worth mentioning that although there was very little to study in Plato's time, some thinkers who preceded him were, in fact, deemed to be philosophers. As was mentioned in chapter 1, probably the first was Thales of Melitus, around 600 BC. Thales might also have been among the earliest of EPrags. At one time in the Asia Minor region where he lived, he had indications of a coming favorable harvest season, so he bought up all the olive presses, and when the good harvest came, he made a fortune. Indications are that Thales was not greedy, but he wanted to demonstrate to the public an aspect of his philosophy—the importance of critical thinking. Sadly, after Thales, there has been a paucity of true pragmatic action among philosophers.

As to my epiphany, it may have been a great revelation or simply a major rationalization. In either case it served to relieve me of the guilty burden I was carrying. For a while I had actually believed that if I did not spend my life in the undying pursuit of the answers sought through the ages, I would be wasting whatever intellectual gifts might have been given to me. Such is one of the challenges of youth, when a good deal of our focus is driven by hormones rather than intellect.

I finally began to appreciate the notion that the world needed architects, policemen, lawyers, doctors, economists, soldiers, factory workers, farmers, scientists, salesmen, retailers, and everyone else who could make life worth living for all of us. It wasn't necessary to be Aristotle. Further, the epiphany provided me with another justification, or perhaps as I indicated, a rationalization—that I really couldn't be much of a philosopher if all I did was study. I later received partial validation from Voltaire, who once said,

> I believe that there never was a creator of a philosophical system who did not confess at the end of his life that he had wasted his time. It must be admitted that the inventors of the mechanical arts have been much more useful to men that the inventors of syllogisms. He, who imagined a ship, towers considerably above him who imagined innate ideas.

Much later as my own philosophy, EP, was being refined, I reflected on what it means to be a philosopher and I concluded that there really were no educational requirements. The only prerequisites were those set out in my definition at the beginning of this chapter. After that, anyone can be legitimately called a philosopher. You, the reader, as well, whether you have a PhD or not. Consider these questions: How many great writers had a PhD in literature? Shakespeare? Dickens? James Joyce? Or any of the Pulitzer Prize winners throughout history? How many great artists had a PhD in art or music? da Vinci? Rembrandt? Picasso? Mozart? Beethoven? Richard Rogers? Cole Porter? They, and philosophers through the ages, all simply had the ability to generate something of value.

Based on the conclusion justified by the foregoing reasoning, I proceeded to live my life in the way I ultimately chose. It has been a conventional life albeit quite interesting, but it afforded me the freedom to be the kind of student and learner that I ultimately realized was the best to be—someone who could learn from life and learn from reading and studying wherever and whenever the opportunity arose. It enabled me, and would have enabled anyone like me, to work toward achieving the fusion of theory and practice that I have come to espouse in my proprietary philosophy, ethical pragmatism.

Chapter 4

Enunciating the Credo

Every one of us is, in the cosmic perspective, precious. If a human disagrees with you, let him live. In a hundred billion galaxies, you will not find another.

—Carl Sagan

The basic and uncompromising premise of ethical pragmatism is that human life has value and that all actions taken in society must be governed by the recognition of that premise. The actions taken by all authorities must be done in a functional manner so as to achieve the goal of the betterment of human existence. In basic terms, ethical pragmatism dictates that all actions in any society should be consistent with doing what works best. What distinguishes ethical pragmatism from nineteenth-century pragmatism, utilitarianism, or ordinary pragmatism is that ethical pragmatism espouses the judicious application of mores, morals, and ethics consistent with human compassion and what we have come to define as individual rights.

In evaluating the premise of ethical pragmatism, it is appropriate to ask several questions. Why does human life have value? Among all living things, why should humans be afforded compassion and individual rights? Why is human life distinguished from, and given a special status over, other forms of life? These are questions that theologians, scientists, and other thinkers have pondered throughout the history of human thought.

In the infinitesimally small part of the universe that we inhabit and call Earth, living organisms abound. These organisms have been here in a multitude of forms for what to us is an incalculable time—certainly millions, perhaps billions of years. At some very recent point during the lengthy existence of these organisms, nature, by design or accident, conferred upon one species, *Homo sapiens*, the ability to influence their own lives, the lives of other living things, and their natural environment. Coupled with certain limited physical attributes, we *Homo sapiens,* or as we colloquially refer to ourselves, human beings, were given a superior form of intelligence.

The attributes given to us—like the ability to reason and communicate among ourselves—enabled us to accomplish things presumably never before known on Earth. From these we were able to create and employ wondrous artifacts. We were able to contemplate lofty ideas and create beautiful things for all our senses to appreciate.

Humans, as no other living thing on Earth, have the ability to address the notion of life itself and make choices on a level not contemplated by nature in all other species of life—flora or fauna. Other organisms merely exist and follow the paths prescribed by nature. Humans have the ability to change what nature has prescribed.

Humans, individually, and perhaps as a species as well, have a finite existence. I do not comment on the duration on Earth of other organisms except to say that it appears to be in the natural order of life on Earth that at some point all organisms must die so that others may live.

Since we arrived at that status we call "human," we have had to make choices, some inadvertently, about which organisms—whether simple cells, plants, animals, or humans—must die in order that we can benefit in some way.

Observe that in societies valuing human life, there seems to be little concern regarding the practice of extinguishing many other living things.

With moral and legal impunity, we consume or destroy vegetation of all kinds. We kill bacteria and other organisms; we kill insects and fish, and with relatively little objection, many other species throughout the animal kingdom.

However, it seems that the higher the potential killing target rises on the evolutionary ladder, the more inhibitions we develop regarding the objects of killing. No one demonstrates opposition to killing ants, mosquitoes, or hornets, but protests are common regarding the slaughter of many animals for food or other by-products of their remains. It appears, therefore, that the more seemingly human traits an animal has (e.g., mammals, primates), the less likely a human is to kill it.

Theologians say that all humans have a soul. How humans acquire a soul is not easily explained. Notwithstanding the difficulty of substantiating such a claim, religion contends that the possession of a soul from whatever source apparently places humans in a different category from all other living things in our universe.

Ethical pragmatism does not rely on religious or, for that matter, purely scientific concepts as the basis for its conclusions. Pragmatism is the watchword, and since every culture in history has distinguished humans from other forms of life, it becomes essential, in a pragmatic sense, to accord human beings some kind of special status.

Human beings are not different simply because they have an opposable thumb. We are uniquely capable in many areas—for example, abstract thought; depth of emotion; aesthetic appreciation; endeavors such as science, art, and music; and even humor! We also can speak.

In a purely scientific analysis, perhaps no living thing should be treated differently from any other living thing. However, we are, in fact, humans, and our basic instincts, principally that of self-preservation, have apparently dictated our placing ourselves in this special category in order to survive. The values that derive from this inherently human cognitive and emotional progression are perhaps the essence of what has come to be known as "human nature."

Thus we, as humans, conclude, in a somewhat self-serving thought process, that humans are different and are entitled to the special classification afforded them in our world. The starting point and foundation of all thoughts in ethical pragmatism is the assumption that the value of human life is the underlying basis of universal morality. This theme persists in this philosophy notwithstanding that the degree of the value of human life has varied throughout history and from culture to culture.

Taking the position that human life has value is not without its complications. Promulgating any belief inevitably raises questions and often provokes controversy. In terms of the value of human life, one might ask if all human lives have the same value, or if killing in any circumstance is ever justified. Some might ask how to define human life, such as when human life begins or ends. These are often troubling issues and sometimes require uncomfortable evaluations. It is significant to note and acknowledge that the concept of human life having value, as well as the philosophy of ethical pragmatism, is not absolute. The ethical component of EP does not require absolute application of the principle, but it does require judicious consideration of it before one reaches a conclusion. Thus, as an example, the fighting of a defensive war or other actions resulting in death can be justified for a greater good.

EP, in its purest application, does not foster using the dogmas produced by engaging in partisan politics, or what this writer refers to as "competitive political activity," nor aligning with any political, industrial, social, religious, or military group. No special interest is ever favored, whether in the United States or elsewhere around the world. EP must always function by approaching all questions and issues completely devoid of the corruption caused by any consideration except merit and intrinsic value.

Being realistic, however, one must acknowledge that even people who adopt EP as their own philosophy will generally continue to participate in the entire spectrum of human activity. This inevitably challenges how we feel about a variety of topics and makes it difficult for us to shed the prejudices that are concomitant to living in a complex, interactive society. EP does not discourage belonging to, or being a part of, a group, organization, religion, or political party, but it is hoped that the basic principles of EP—those of objectivity, impartiality, and fairness—will always be used as standards. Ethical pragmatism can exist and thrive amidst this apparent situational contradiction as long as we remember that we should never compromise principles but always be willing to compromise positions.

Similarly, except for purposes of explanation and illustration, EP tries to avoid, and does not embrace, generic labels attributed to human actions, thoughts, or beliefs. There are many categories, labels, and designations that often are used in a pejorative sense or in an attempt to discredit the proponent or opponent of a position. We have all heard and read them. Among these terms are people accused of being pro-labor, pro-management, permissive, soft on crime, or in the religious right. Some labels and categories include agnostic, anarchist, atheist, bleeding heart, capitalist, communist, conservative, demagogue, fascist, leftist, liberal, Nazi, progressive, reactionary, redneck, rightist, socialist, and others. EP finds such designations counterproductive, since EP is concerned only with what works, not with what something or someone may be called or because of who supports or opposes it. There is no indication of there being a dispute between the left and the right when the wheel was being invented! No one should ever be labeled for expressing an opinion. Only the opinion itself is open to fair comment as to its soundness.

Thus, the credo of ethical pragmatism requires the application of reason and common sense in order to produce rational behavior and action. In this way we can seek and find the best method of achieving the most desirable goals of mankind for the greatest number of people.

The following have been proved to be useful to EP (alphabetically): accountability, applied technology, common sense (of course), competency, critical thinking, disclosure, due process of law, goal-oriented solutions and actions, honor, integrity, liberty, merit, order, recognition of reality, respect for others, science, tolerance (both political and social), transparency, truth, and, after judicious application of its principles, violence when it is used to save lives.

To give an idea of what EP loathes and rejects, consider the following: bigotry, corruption, discrimination (unjustified), fraud, hypocrisy, incompetency, intolerance, mendacity, religious extremism, terrorism, and unjustified violence.

EP is skeptical about disingenuous euphemisms, hyperbole, political correctness, social engineering, and spin (in the contemporary competitive political sense).

In terms of EP, it is necessary to apply critical thinking in order to distinguish among some practices that are principally negative and others that may have positive or redeeming features. A good example is the difference between stereotyping and profiling. Stereotyping is not evidence based. It involves the unjustified leap of faith rejected by EP in the formulation of opinions that attribute characteristics of a group to an individual or characteristics of an individual to a group. It is often a form of prejudice. On the other hand, profiling, as it is known in the current age of societal threats, can be a valuable tool in the hands of law enforcement when judiciously applied. Stereotyping results in a conclusion while profiling seeks answers before an evidence based conclusion can be drawn. It is in the *application* of these two practices that the distinction needs to be drawn. Making that distinction is aided by the use of common sense.

Appreciating the credo of EP as to the value of human life, the necessity of acting objectively and other components expressed in this book is important. It is, however, also important to appreciate that Ethical pragmatism is not an absolute, rigid philosophy but a living, tolerant, evolving way of dealing with all human challenges, endeavors, and issues. To that end, it must be understood that any position, ideology, or belief expressed, espoused, or embraced in ethical pragmatism can and should be modified when one is provided with justification consistent with the basic principles of EP. If it works or will work, EPrags will support it. If it does not work, EPrags will urge improving or replacing it.

Highlights of Chapter 4

1. Human life has value.
2. Ethical pragmatism means addressing everything by
   A. Being sure of the facts.
   B. Ignoring all labels, ideologies, political beliefs, and outside influences in order to
      i. Determine the goal.
      ii. Find the best way to reach the goal.

Chapter 5

Foundation of the Credo

Life is not a problem to be solved, but a reality to be experienced.
—Soren Kierkegaard

The underlying premise of EP as previously described cannot be emphasized enough. This premise produces the basic tenet of EP: that human life has value. The basis for the premise and thus the tenet has been discussed previously, so it is not necessary to revisit all aspects of the thought processes leading to its formulation. As has been discussed, in order to implement EP, one *must* accept that human life is distinguishable from other living things and that reasonable measures and actions must be undertaken to preserve, protect, nurture, and prolong it. But *why* must it be accepted? The answer is no more complicated than this: it is because if you do not believe it, you cannot be an ethical pragmatist.

Since times even before the ancient Greeks, thinkers and philosophers have been searching for answers, but in some sense, there really are no answers except those we provide to the questions we ourselves are asking. With all of the "whys" and millions of other words written, with the countless hours of pondering, discussing, and arguing, no conclusions have ever been reached without making some assumption. Make any statement or supply any answer to any question, and you can start an endless series of whys. This occurs because until you make a choice—that is, an assumption— there is no answer to why? that will not generate another why? Once the assumption is made and stated in an answer, the whys have no more validity.

I revere science. It may be the only repository of absolutes we know, and even science may suffer from incursions of relativism (see, e.g., the works of Albert Einstein). We define science as an enterprise or discipline that gathers and organizes knowledge about everything in the universe. How it differs from what we know as philosophy is that science draws testable conclusions—conclusions that can be verified—and those conclusions or findings can be used to make absolute predictions. For example, water freezes at 0 degrees Celsius and will at all times in the future freeze at 0 degrees Celsius. There is nothing comparable in the study or pursuit of philosophy or any of the other bodies of knowledge and study. When someone uses the term "not an exact science" in referring to some endeavor, it does not acknowledge the truth about that endeavor ... the truth being it is not a science at all. Political "science," psychology, sociology, a variety of other "...ology's," and all the social "sciences" are not science or sciences. If any terms could be used to find a category for them, perhaps my own terms would suffice. I would prefer to call them something like "quasi-sciences" or "shadow-sciences."

My purpose in addressing the issue of the various terms used to describe these endeavors is to point out that working in those areas is simply not scientific. Consequently, no conclusions can ever be absolute. This is not bad; it is simply a reality. Thus, in the study of philosophy or the attempt to reach a philosophical conclusion of any kind, searching for the verification will always be fruitless. The answers to those eternal questions cannot be found in nature or in natural law. It would be wonderful to turn over a rock and find the "truth" or any absolute about our exercises in thought, but it cannot happen. There are no ways of finding "truth" or any absolute standard. Unending speculation and theorizing in a purely academic setting can serve many purposes, but to a society aching to function it can only lead to chaos. In an atmosphere of chaos there is no order, and the establishment of order is necessary to commence any civilization. At some point, a choice must be made to depart from theory and start toward practice.

We begin by abandoning the search for absolutes. Only in relative terms—relative to the assumptions we ourselves make—can we formulate valid syllogisms and arrive at sound conclusions. What I have come to believe and what is an essential component of EP, is that some assumption based on subjectivity must be made at some point to achieve functionality.

Think of riding on an object that has always been orbiting the earth and presumably will continue to do so. Like most philosophical exercises without a hypothesis, all you will do on the object is continue to orbit or, as we say, "go around in circles." In order for you to end your eternal circling, you need to pick a point to get off. The point where you get off is your assumption—your hypothesis—and that is where and when you can begin to make progress.

Following that move, the starting point in EP becomes the act of adopting the tenet that human life has value. This may be *my* starting point, but it might not be yours. Nor is this tenet based entirely on logic. Where does it come from? Well, it could come from anyone who believes as I do. In this case it comes from me. Adopting this tenet may not be scientifically sound or universally accepted. I certainly cannot prove scientifically that human life has value. The tenet is simply derived from a rational thought process to serve as a hypothesis upon which to structure a model for human existence. It is based on common sense.

The tenet about life having value may be challenged by those who think only in absolute terms, by subscribers to certain objectivist beliefs, or by others, but it need not be defended in the same sense that we need not defend our feelings. Our feelings are what they are, and no one can dispute or dismiss them. Similarly, the tenet cannot be successfully challenged, because it is a matter of personal belief, preference, and choice.

I acknowledge that the tenet is based on a premise that is subjectively derived; it is an assumption/presumption *chosen* by ethical pragmatists as the foundation of the credo *that all human life has value.* Making such a choice is completely consistent with the ultimate belief in, and application of, the philosophy, because, as was stated above, it is the only *pragmatic* way in which the philosophy can begin. Without the underlying premise, the belief, and ultimately, the choice, all one would have is a theoretical, abstract, conceptual exercise. The choice itself is the point of embarkation (or disembarkation as in the "orbiting" analogy) on what will be a journey of adventure, evolution, service, and gratification. The selection, adoption, and application of the basic tenet begin the implementation of ethical pragmatism.

It is appropriate to accept that there may be cultures, peoples, groups, or individuals who have beliefs to the contrary—that human life is valueless, for example. Whatever they are or whatever they may be called, they are not ethical pragmatists.

Chapter 6

Common Sense

Common sense is the genius of humanity.
　　　　　　　　—Johann Wolfgang von Goethe

It is a thousand times better to have common sense without education than to have education without common sense.
　　　　　　　　—Robert Green Ingersoll

Science is simply common sense at its best, that is, rigidly accurate in observation, and merciless to fallacy in logic.
　　　　　　　　—Thomas Huxley

Ethical pragmatism is the common sense philosophy. It is considered to be the common sense philosophy for two reasons. The first is that following its principles throughout any exercise requires the application of common sense. The second reason, which is explained in the following paragraphs, is that common sense is needed, and used, to make the necessary choices that create the core of the philosophy.

As was previously stated, the hypothesis that human life has value is the basis of ethical pragmatism. As was also stated, in my view, it is not necessary to defend this hypothesis, because it follows a choice that we ourselves make. Challenging this would be akin to challenging what someone feels. There is no wrong or right about feelings. They are simply felt. Choosing the hypothesis that human life has value is more like a feeling than a scientific conclusion. It is chosen because common sense tells us, or makes us feel, that it is right. Once having made the choice and adopting the premise for the philosophy, all debate ends. In this eternal, infinite universe of ours, the only way to avoid the circular, endless explorations of any premise is to make a choice and move on.

The choice we make about human life having value is admittedly subjective. There are always those who pose challenges to any belief, and when philosophy is involved, the challenges are almost as infinite as the universe itself. Again, my view is that an ethical pragmatist need not answer the challenges, because the belief in the chosen hypothesis alone justifies the foundation of the philosophy.

That having been said, I will continue to say that social intercourse often compels us to afford our colleagues, neighbors, friends, and relatives the courtesy of some type of explanation for the choice. This is true even if the explanation is not fully accepted as a justification in the same *sense* used in a philosophical debate. The explanation is, of course, common sense.

Common sense is the watchword/phrase and polestar of the hypothesis and, more broadly, of the philosophy itself. Without common sense we cannot have wisdom, because wisdom is derived from common sense. Wisdom is the compound produced by merging experience *with* common sense. I should note, however, that based on my observations concerning contemporary society, what has long been considered common sense is now, in reality, quite uncommon. Voltaire made this same observation (*Dictionnaire Philosophique*, 1764), and others may have done so as well. A phrase like "uncommon sense" would seem to make more *sense*. Nevertheless, the phrase, and the title of this chapter, has been in use for so long and its meaning so universally understood that it seems more pragmatic to keep it. Therefore, the rest of this chapter and ensuing references to "common sense" will deferentially continue its use.

The Oxford Dictionaries (*OED Online*. February, 2016. *Oxford University Press*) define common sense as "good sense and sound judgment in practical matters," while Merriam-Webster (*Merriam-Webster.com*. 2015) says that common sense is "the ability to think and behave in a reasonable way and to make good decisions." Both seem correct to me.

Aristotle is first credited with using the term, or the Greek equivalent of the term, and the first to define the concept. (See *De Anima* Book III, chapter 2, 425a27; *De Anima* III.7, 431b; *De memoria et reminiscentia* 1450a; *De Partibus Animalium* IV.10, 686a; *Metaphysics* I.1 981b; *Historia Animalium* I.3, 489a. See Gregorić, 2007.)

Throughout history others have alluded to it. This is what Rene Descartes had to say about *Bon Sens*, here translated from the original French (italics mine):

> Good Sense is, of all things among men, the most equally distributed; for every one thinks himself so abundantly provided with it, that those even who are the most difficult to satisfy in everything else, do not usually desire a larger measure of this quality than they already possess. And in this it is not likely that all are mistaken: the conviction is rather to be held as testifying that the power of judging a right and of distinguishing truth from error, which is properly what is called good sense or reason, is by nature equal in all men; and that the diversity of our opinions, consequently, does not arise from some being endowed with a larger share of reason than others, but solely from this, that we conduct our thoughts along different ways, and do not fix our attention on the same objects. *For to be possessed of a vigorous mind is not enough; the prime requisite is rightly to apply it.* The greatest minds, as they are capable of the highest achievements, are open likewise to the greatest aberrations; and those who travel very slowly may yet make far greater progress, provided they keep always to the straight road, than those who, while they run, forsake it.

Common sense tells us that ignorance is bad, corruption is bad, incompetence is bad, hypocrisy is bad, mendacity is bad, pain is bad, suffering is bad, and cruelty is bad. It tells us that saving and prolonging lives is good. It tells us that peace is better than war, tolerance is better than bigotry, thrift is better than waste, prosperity is better than poverty, health is better than sickness, freedom is better than subjugation, and order is better than chaos.

Pragmatism has a kinship with common sense and depends on it for the bulk of its reasoning and conclusions. However, people do not always agree about what is sensible. Many would argue that one cannot learn common sense; it is an innate quality. Although people have thought about and searched for the origins of common sense quite a bit, there is still no indication of where it comes from.

We can only guess as to how we get common sense. Maybe we are born with it. Maybe some faculty we have enables us to recognize common sense in action when we are young, and that same faculty develops as we grow and becomes more and more a part of us as we mature. This is what the Scottish philosopher James Beattie said about it in the eighteenth century (*"An Essay on the Nature and Immutability of Truth,"* p. 40):

> [T]hat power of the mind which perceives truth, or commands belief, not by progressive argumentation, but by an instantaneous, instinctive, and irresistible impulse; derived neither from education nor from habit, but from nature; acting independently on our will, whenever its object is presented, according to an established law, and therefore properly called Sense; and acting in a similar manner upon all, or at least upon a great majority of mankind, and therefore properly called Common Sense.

It is clear that not everyone has, and is able to, exercise common sense. Common sense is not bound to education. It is more closely linked to a kind of enlightenment that some have regardless of their backgrounds or stations in life. Somehow, reason and logic are spontaneously generated in the minds of some and are conspicuously missing in the minds of others. Whatever common sense is, or however we get it, to effectively apply the principles of EP in actual practice, people need to have common sense, whether by birth or acquisition, and they also need to use it.

Although it is doubtful that one can take a course that teaches common sense, two works are recommended relating to common sense. In addition to their titles, these two works exhibit common sense (or the lack thereof) in their content. The two relevant works are from two completely different eras. They are Thomas Paine's *Common Sense* (1776) and *The Death of Common Sense* (1994), by Phillip K. Howard. Both of these men might have unknowingly been EPrags when they wrote their works. Paine wrote in order to convince the American colonists to seek independence from England, and he advanced numerous pragmatic arguments to support his position. Howard wrote about the blunders of government institutions and how government bureaucracy is operating in a manner inimical to the interests of its citizens. Howard made astute analyses that open the door to pragmatic suggestions for resolving some of the issues addressed in his book.

One way of testing if common sense is being used in any given situation is to apply the standards of EP. After acknowledging regard for human life and tolerance, you must determine that your actions are consistent with the philosophy. Do this in two parts:

1. Ask yourself if you have the impartial, objective, and accurate facts.
2. Ask yourself, in the light of reality, if what you contemplate doing will actually produce the desired result.

If you have answered "yes" twice, you are on your way.

Chapter 7

Cause and Effect

Life is a perpetual instruction in cause and effect.
> —Ralph Waldo Emerson

Shallow men believe in luck or in circumstance. Strong men believe in cause and effect.
> —Ralph Waldo Emerson

A designer knows he has achieved perfection not when there is nothing left to add, but when there is nothing left to take away.
> —Antoine de Saint-Exupery

I never dreamed about success, I worked for it.
> —Estee Lauder

At this point it should be clear that EP seeks a practical way to approach all circumstances in life without relying on the emotions that mislead us. The manner must be devoid of the corrupting influences of ideologies, labels, partisan politics, religious dogma, and special interests. What this really means is that we are seeking to identify both a *cause* and an *effect* with total objectivity.

In terms of effects, there are two categories. One is an effect that already exists. As to this existing effect, whether good or bad, we would seek to identify its cause; that is, the reason or reasons we have the effect. If we determine that the existing effect is good, we would celebrate the cause and support, perpetuate, or enhance it. If we determine that the existing effect is bad, we would consider changing or eliminating the cause.

As to the second category, an effect that does not yet exist but that we want to produce, we would have to devise a cause; that is, the instrument that will bring about the desired effect. We often think of this as finding a solution to a problem or innovating something creative to bring about an entirely new set of circumstances.

These causes and effects encompass all realms of our existence in social, political, scientific, commercial, and artistic areas and even more specifically in human relations, government, health care, research, manufacturing, construction, agriculture, finance, education, the professions, the communications media, and even leisure and the general quality of life.

Is there a practical way to examine the body of material comprising the causes and effects? I think there is.

Starting early in my adult life, I struggled to find some method of using my brain and senses efficiently in order to deal appropriately with the more challenging decisions I had to make. In searching, I tried to follow the sequence of my thoughts when I was well rested, feeling good, and thinking straight. As a consequence of recognizing the kind of thinking I had been doing unconsciously, I identified, and then formally adopted, a simple thought process consisting of a sequence of steps. These are the steps I have used and through the years have tried to spread to those I have mentored.

With regard to any stimulus of the senses, I do the following:

Observe, Analyze, Evaluate, and Conclude

I use this for everything, whether it is to solve an extremely challenging problem or simply to watch a movie, eat a cookie, or look at the sky. Every sense we have provides us with something to observe, analyze, evaluate, and reach a conclusion about, even if the conclusion is *not to conclude*, at least for the present.

In most of the things we do, we actually pass unconsciously through these four steps, and often the steps overlap or merge with one another. From the time we awaken, our days are routinely filled with conclusions that unknowingly flow from such a process. Take two examples:

1. You hear a ringing sound. You *observe* what it is and that it comes from your alarm clock. You *analyze* that it is meant to awaken you so that you will not be late for work. You *evaluate* that if you shut it off and return to sleep, you will be late for work. You therefore *conclude* that you will shut off the alarm, get out of bed, and prepare for the day.
2. You are walking at night in a deserted downtown area. After turning a corner, you hear a gunshot. You *observe* the sound of the gun's report and from where it came—back around the corner. You *analyze* that this may be a felony in progress or some other occurrence, and your curiosity is raised. You *evaluate* that if you go back around the corner, you may be in great danger, but if you go quickly on your way, you will likely avert danger. You *conclude* to go very quickly on your way.

In the theoretically philosophical world, each of the above steps itself can be observed, analyzed, and evaluated before one reaches a conclusion if one ever gets that far along. Just consider what William James would do with the observation step alone. He states that any cognition consists of two parts—sensation and perception. James explains that the function of sensation is that of mere acquaintance with a fact, while the function of perception is knowledge about the same fact (*The Principles of Psychology*, 1890).

One could do what James and many of his colleagues did—similarly dissect the other steps as well. In my view this is not helpful to engaging an issue. The manner of using my thinking process does not require anything beyond what the actual words of the four steps describe. The words are clear enough to trigger the series of thoughts that get me prepared for action.

As I stated, in order to apply the principles of EP to real circumstances, it is desirable, if not necessary, to follow some thought process. One may follow mine, one similar to mine, or some other orderly method of identifying the issue and determining what goal is sought. Preparing for action requires thought. The first step is critical. I cannot emphasize this enough. To observe with any meaning, it is necessary to strip away all emotions and recognize reality. Whatever the reality, it must be accurately acknowledged and accepted, because if you are wrong about the facts, nothing positive can follow. On the other hand, if you are right about the facts, the analysis and evaluation will flow much more easily and the intended goal becomes attainable.

We are now trying to prepare for action; that is, devise a cause. It may be to formulate a business plan, design a patentable mechanism, or create anything else that can be imagined. It may be to find a solution to an existing problem or to develop something entirely new. Whatever it is, it becomes necessary to project the consequences (effect) of the cause. In using the principles of EP, it ultimately falls upon us to make the overview evaluation and prediction regarding efficacy of the cause, meaning basically, "Will it work?" (See note 1 to chapter 7 at the end of this chapter.)

When we say, "Will it work?" we are examining cause and effect. This question has been the subject of considerable thought throughout the ages, so I feel some digression may be in order. Once again, I admonish—do not be put off by what you are about to read, as much of the following contains theoretical exercises that, although admirable and in some cases useful, ultimately have little, if any, significance in applying EP.

"Cause" and "effect" together *cause* a great deal of material to be written. The words are found in various forms throughout our culture and literature. There is a whole body of thought known as "causality." We have the Eastern concept of karma, the Granger test in economics, and the Ishikawa diagrams in product design. Then there are the "occasionalists," who contend that nothing in human reality is the cause of anything else, because God has already determined the effect.

Some great thinkers and philosophers have addressed the notion of cause and effect. Aristotle felt there were four causes: material, formal, efficient, and final. In Spinoza's *Ethics*, he poses the following axiom: "From a given determinate cause an effect necessarily follows; and, on the other hand, if no determinate cause can be given, it is impossible that an effect can follow." Spinoza's axiom may seem obvious (for which I am grateful), but in elaborating he takes the reader on a very long journey involving much more complex commentary. David Hume suggests the idea that cause and effect may not even be connected, and John Stuart Mill seems to have subscribed to that theory as well.

Georg Hegel believed that we perceive a cause only after we see its effect and perceive an effect only after we discover its cause. Just to emphasize how lost we can get in using these simple terms, consider the kind of verbiage Hegel used, regardless of the original language, in writing about such terms (*Part One, Encyclopaedia of Philosophical Sciences: The Logic*, 1830):

> [T]he distinction of cause and effect is introduced by the understanding into an essentially homogeneous continuum, but reason reveals that they are not metaphysically distinct because distinctions such as cause and effect occur as moments within the dialectic as functions of our effort to understand experience, but in the final moment of a particular dialectical process we see that the distinctions we posited are moments within a larger whole.

Whew! Did Hegel think that anyone would really appreciate the usefulness of this? As profound as it may be, it means absolutely nothing to EP and the application of common sense.

Finally, here is the belief of John Dewey, who was actually considered to be a "pragmatist." He wrote that cause and effect (means and ends) are not metaphysically distinct realities, but integrally related moments or stages within a process. And this is from a "pragmatist," no less!

Much of what one can read—and there is very much to read—about cause and effect should be considered from an EP point of view to be nothing more than dialectical legerdemain. It may be commendable that the participants through their studies and works have said what they have said and done what they have done, but none of it bears any relationship to the implementing of EP.

It is imperative that before embracing this philosophy and attempting to apply its principles to the real world, we recognize and acknowledge that we are human beings. This means that we should not be behaving like sheep. We are not all as smart as others or as educated as some, but absent some pathology or aberrance we all have enough intelligence to make basic realistic observations if we train ourselves to ignore emotions and other damaging influences.

Only after being sure of the facts—even ultimately embracing the harshness of what is examined—and then applying the thought process, are we ready to create the cause, whether it is a model, paradigm, plan, project, or any action requiring a decision.

The entire process leading to the creation of the cause that will bring the desired effect must be kept pure. It cannot be stated too often—the process must not be contaminated by the emotional influences previously mentioned or by associating the steps in the process or the projected effect of the process with those who support or oppose it. In striving for a thorough evaluation of our work, we may reach out to the academic or scientific communities or simply to our friends and families for confirmation of our factual assumptions ... but, in the end, the product of the process must be judged only on its intrinsic worth. Merit alone is the standard, and common sense is the guiding force.

Notes to Chapter 7

The author has included two sections in these notes for the purpose of demonstrating structured applications of EP. Section 1 involves a formula. It is acknowledged that most times when formulae are introduced, confusion may occur. It is hoped that what follows in section 1 will be useful in applying the principles of EP, but it is not necessary to assimilate the following content in order to implement the philosophy. Section 2 provides a simple suggestion as to how one can evaluate a career move.

Section 1: In Search of *Ugo* (Pronounced *Hugo*)

Much of what we do on a daily basis is not planned or contemplated in any way before we act. We do things by rote, from habit, or by following our instincts. But whenever we pause long enough to think before we act, we really need to ask ourselves the question "Will this work?" The question/concept may be phrased in various ways, but the idea is the same. You are essentially asking yourself if what you are about to do makes sense. Whatever you are considering requires using a thought process that facilitates making the determination. Whether the thought process is mine (observation, analysis, evaluation, and conclusion) or some other sensible method, the entire process must be performed without our being inhibited or misled by emotions or other corrupting influences.

Although objectivity must prevail throughout the process, it is necessary to address those steps in the process to which objectivity must be applied. For example, in finding what will work, we first have to identify the goal we are seeking. This is more difficult than it sounds, but after we assimilate a few techniques and apply them, the process becomes easier and eventually second nature.

Often a cause will produce an effect that is only part of the way toward what should actually be achieved; that is, reaching what may be regarded as a preliminary goal but not a genuine ultimate goal as some would define it. Although the basic hypothesis of EP is that human life has value, the ultimate goal in an EP exercise is not the abstract notion of what is good for humanity. Seeking the best things for humanity and honoring human life are assumed in any exercise, so the ultimate goal in an EP exercise will always, of necessity, be contextual.

As an example, suppose a group of community leaders were meeting to address a challenge. This could be in any area, such as traffic, crime, health, environment, or others. What goal are the participants seeking? If one of the participants said, "My goal is the betterment of all mankind," most would laugh, or someone might say, "Everyone in this room is seeking that; now let's get down to business!" Remember, EP is a relativist philosophy. There are no absolutes, so the ultimate goal for our purposes is one that may fall far short of the lofty achievement of serving all mankind. Nevertheless, the group's goal might provide a worthy target, serving as the effect desired in the set of circumstances under consideration.

Following the foregoing illustration, at this point it is helpful to define some terms and name them for ease in analyzing and assimilating the process. As has been stated, in applying EP, the ultimate goal is not the lofty, humanitarian, perhaps even utopian, final status one would describe in a perfect world. In EP, the ultimate goal (UGo) is the final destination *in the process*; it is the effect being sought in the overall cause/effect equation.

Along the way, however, there may be interim goals that lead to UGo. The penultimate goal may be an attainment just before getting to the end, but still leaving something to be done. This is called "PG-1" (not named for penultimate), meaning pre-goal number 1. The further we get from Ugo, the higher the pre-goal number. For example, in a given project we may have to reach several levels before we can produce UGo. The first level, accomplishment, or pre-goal might be PG-3. The next along the way would be PG-2, and the last before reaching UGo would be PG-1.

Additionally, as was previously stated, there are often differences of opinion as to the desirability of the results even after participants acknowledge that the process was sound and resulted in the formulation of something that actually will work. When this happens, breaking down the components with an organized approach naming the steps in the process has value in helping to give a clearer overview to all who participate.

Let's take a relatively simple example that involves finding a remedy for some threat to society, such as inoculating a population against an impending disease ("the program"). Here we can apply the EP process.

There are two sides to the issue. Those in favor of the program argue that everyone must be inoculated; those opposed to the program believe it is not necessary, it is too costly, and it will not be effective in preventing the disease.

First, we have to observe the facts. What percentage of the population is likely to be stricken? What will be the severity of the disease? What will be the effectiveness of the program? How much will the program cost? All this process requires that one take a cold, objective look at all the available scientific and economic data in both observation and analysis. Any analysis allows one to assess the credibility of what is observed—in this case, the scientific projections, the logistics, and the costs. When it is ascertained that the facts are accurate, every aspect of the entire program has to be evaluated before a conclusion can be reached. What actions will produce what consequences?

Here are the two views in this example. One favors inoculation, and one is opposed. Let us assume that the facts show that only 10 percent of the population will be infected and that the inoculation has nearly 100 percent effectiveness. The only issue therefore is cost. The facts further indicate that even with 10 percent infected, there will be no fatalities and everyone infected can be treated, but the *cost of treatment* will be far less than the cost of the program. It then becomes clear that each course of action (or inaction) will produce a result. The observation and analysis steps produced the facts permitting the ensuing evaluation. With the evaluation complete and projections made based on the evaluation, a conclusion must now be drawn. In order to draw the conclusion (the decision), there has to be consensus, if not unanimity, of thought. Now we have the debate.

The proponents of the program might think that the inoculation is the goal (effect) and that getting the funding is its cause. This is wrong, as I will show in the next paragraph. This would skew any debate by making inoculation the center of controversy, when even those opposed to inoculation in this specific situation might be generally in favor of inoculation under different circumstances.

In applying the principles of EP, any approach to a topic requires that the first priority is to identify what we have named the *ultimate goal*, or UGo. In this case, the ultimate goal is not whether or not to inoculate the population; here it is really a goal that sounds in the nature of ethical pragmatism, which is the preservation of life and life's quality for the greatest number. But this case is really more concrete because it applies specifically to a particular, present threat—a disease. Inoculating the population is merely a preliminary goal that EP would call a pre-goal. There may be many pre-goals. Since inoculating is the nearest pre-goal from the ultimate goal, EP would designate it PG-1. For those in favor of inoculation, getting the funding would be the next nearest pre-goal, or PG-2. Those in favor of the program might conclude that PG-2 (funding) is the cause and PG-1 (inoculation) is the effect. Again, this would be wrong. Although PG-1 is an effect of PG-2, PG-1 (inoculation) is not the ultimate goal. The ultimate goal (UGo) would be the *effect* of PG-1.

Those opposing the program, however, might argue that although the cause, PG-2, results in the effect PG-1, PG-1 does not produce UGo because, as the acknowledged facts bear out, the cost of inoculating will be more than the cost of treating the 10 percent affected. The opposition might argue that paying for inoculating 100 percent of the people is an unreasonable financial imposition. It will impact the quality of life of 100 percent of the population, while only 10 percent of the population will become sick and can be treated at a much lower cost. Since UGo is not reached by PG-2 and PG-1, this is not pragmatic from the opponents' position.

Proponents of the program could argue that UGo is reached as a result of PG-2 and PG-1, because 10 percent of the people are spared having to suffer the disease and treatment and the cost to the 100 percent will impact quality of life for all far less than having the disease will for the unfortunate 10 percent.

As you can see, objectivity and impartiality are challenged by a value judgment. But the purpose of this illustration is not to select a side or make a value judgment; it is to facilitate identifying what it is that is under consideration.

If it is believed that inoculating or not inoculating was the ultimate goal, the debate would be impeded by focusing on the issue of inoculation rather than on the effect of any action on the entire community from every aspect—including overall cost, who would pay, who would be most likely to suffer, inconvenience to all, and other factors.

Therefore, in the approach to any issue, it is beneficial to identify UGo, PG-1, PG-2, and so on in order to perceive what actions are precipitating which results during the process. This approach allows one to distinguish between the two following examples:

$$PG\text{-}3 > PG\text{-}2 = PG\text{-}1 \text{ (incorrect)}$$
$$PG\text{-}3 > PG\text{-}2 > PG\text{-}1 = UGo \text{ (correct)}$$

In the first example, the cause and effect between PG-3 and PG-2 were accomplished, as they were between PG-2 and PG-1. The problem is that PG-1 was not the desired final result of the process. In this case one has lost sight of UGo, the ultimate goal.

In the second example, the cause and effect process leads all the way to UGo, thus completing the process and attaining the desired result.

Section 2: Career Move Outline

As has been stated, it is not necessary to adopt the formula of section 1, or for that matter any formula, in applying the principles of EP. However, it is necessary to approach any issue in an orderly manner. When government officials are dealing with issues like ratifying a treaty or making determinations about such things as nuclear weapons, the world economy, or our environment, the process is understandably more complex. When we as individuals address an issue, the process may be simpler, but the basic strategies apply.

As an illustration of how one might deal with a common everyday challenge, the following outline is offered as a guide in the situation in which someone is contemplating a career move. This may be a first job, a comparison among job offers or possibilities, or a comparison between a current job and another position. The following illustration is an outline for rating comparable positions on a scale from one to ten. The writer uses a lined paper pad with pros on one side and cons on the other or scores on different sides. Any organized technique that works for the reader will suffice. Simply rate the various categories and add up the results. Remember, this is just a suggested manner of dealing with any given situation that calls for some thought before a decision is made.

Comparable Position Rating Scale 1-10

Analysis 1 = sum total versus sum total
Analysis 2 = ratings of 1–5 are negative (cons); ratings of 6–10 are positives (pros); total pros and cons versus total pros and cons

1. Financial compensation (present)
2. Financial compensation (ultimate/high end)
3. Opportunity to advance compared to other positions
4. Status (present)

5. Status (future)
6. Job security
7. Intellectual stimulation
8. Sense of achievement and reward (subjective)
9. Sense of achievement and reward (recognition by others)
10. Fringe benefits/perquisites (health plan, vacations, etc.)
11. Your time (hours spent on a daily basis—total, starting, ending …)
12. Your time (night/weekend work, days off, flexibility, own schedule)
13. Commuting factors (time, difficulty, expense)
14. Physical conditions—interior (your office or other workplace, safety, comforts and amenities)
15. Physical conditions—exterior (parking, proximity to restaurants, shopping, safety, other services)
16. Social aspects—interior (relationship with staff, colleagues, superiors)
17. Social aspects—exterior (opportunity for social contact)
18. Competency for position (rate at 10 if perfectly qualified, less if over- or underqualified)

End of Part One

In part 1 the author has tried to explain the philosophy of ethical pragmatism and justify it in rational terms. But since EP is meant to work for you, the reader, in the real world, it is necessary to isolate the significant components of the philosophy and its process so that it can be applied to actual circumstances in your life.

If you focus on the aspects of EP described in the preceding chapters and use them effectively, EP will help you. Think about it. Start by accepting nothing on its surface and making no assumptions about anything. Use your mind to challenge everything for the purpose of reaching the reality of the situation—the unabashed true and actual facts you need to have in order to proceed. Be honest with yourself. This realization of the truth may be uncomfortable, but it is necessary.

After you have the facts, do the analysis and evaluation. If you are being sensible and objective, you should be able to conclude which cause will result in which effect. The cause you choose must be the one that will bring about the goal you are seeking in the best possible way. Any method you employ to use EP can work. It may be as simple as writing the pros and cons on two sides of a lined paper pad. It is how you think that counts.

This manner of thinking pertains to all the situations in your life, whether you are acting just for yourself or on behalf of others in your family, among your friends, in your community, in your government, or at your work. There are many examples. What is the reality of the relationship you now have with someone? Are you often upset but suppress your feelings? What about your present or future job? Do you need a change? Will it improve your circumstances? What about choosing a mate who may be your partner for life? Are you really thinking about the future, or are you succumbing to the gratification of satisfying only your present needs? Are you trying to buy a car? A house? Rent an apartment? Find a doctor or dentist? Vote? Make a decision for your employer? Determine your course of action as you serve in government?

All of the above situations, and more, are candidates for invoking the guiding parts of EP so that you bring the most important factor to bear on your actions—common sense.

Part 2 of this book will try to give insights into some potential uses of EP—how and where EP might be used and what I hope you will find to be some interesting things to consider in the realm of EP.

While reading, please always keep in mind that aside from the notion that human life has value, ethical pragmatism is characterized by three simple rules:

1. The recognition and acceptance of the observed factual reality of everything—without embellishment, compromise, or self-deception
2. The disregard of all labels, ideologies, dogmas, persuasions, prejudices, and corrupting emotions
3. The objective, impartial focus on the intrinsic merit of what is under consideration in order to determine what works best

PART 2

Potpourri

Introduction to Part 2

As was previously stated, ethical pragmatism requires objective, impartial, and honest observations of what is perceived. This means facing reality regardless of the pain, discomfort, inconvenience, or embarrassment such reality causes. Having the true, unmitigated facts before considering any matter is completely essential to a philosophy that seeks to fashion a cause that will produce the desired effect. Not having the accurate facts before acting is tantamount to erecting a skyscraper on quicksand.

Some of the chapters in part 2 try to fairly assess facts in real-life situations so that an example can be used to demonstrate how EP can work. The conclusions about facts in this book may require modification when one attempts to actually approach a topic, but I have tried to come as close as possible for illustration purposes.

Part 2 contains chapters that are somewhat general and others that are issue specific. It also contains a few other things. Whereas part 1 deals principally with the philosophy itself and is relevant to all times and places, part 2 is written in terms of the mores and outlooks prevailing at the time of publication. As a result, the issues and topics may soon lose relevance. Nevertheless, the concepts will always have meaning.

Once again, please do not attribute any ideological, partisan, or special-interest motives to the content in this book, as I have attempted to be totally impartial and unbiased. All references to events, people, customs, and cultures, as well as all examples and illustrations, are solely for the purpose of demonstrating how EP might work to in order to serve the best interests of humanity.

Chapter 8

Were They EPrags?

Be practical as well as generous in your ideals. Keep your eyes on the stars, but remember to keep your feet on the ground.
—Theodore Roosevelt

I am only one, but I am one. I cannot do everything, but I can do something. And because I cannot do everything, I will not refuse to do the something that I can do.
—Edward Everett Hale

In chapter 2 you read about inadvertent pragmatism and how it differs from EP. The reason it differs is that no conscious thought process is involved. If a conscious thought process is used, actions completely consistent with EP can be taken by people who never heard of it. In fact, some of these people might qualify to be EPrags in almost everything they do, and others may exhibit EPrag tendencies in only one act. Politicians, industrialists, educators, farmers, soldiers, artists, and athletes may be whatever they are in almost everything they do, but they may, in just one lone circumstance, rise to the level of ethical pragmatism.

There is another type of action that purports to be pragmatism but in reality is not. Some people or groups devise a scheme for gain without contemplating the consequences of the scheme. In a short-sighted view of the situation, the results may be temporarily beneficial, so they seem pragmatic, but in the end there is a negative, often disastrous result. Classic examples of this phenomenon are reigns of despots. Early on, it may seem pragmatic to incarcerate or kill political opponents, but generally the perpetrators pay a big price, often by paying the extreme penalty. Similarly, it may seem pragmatic to lie, cheat, or steal for gain, but the true results of such actions are eventually negative. In EP, this kind of conduct is called "illusory pragmatism" because what seems pragmatic on the surface is merely an illusion.

The following are examples of known figures whose pragmatic acts seem to have been consistent with EP standards, although the philosophy that now has a name and a definition was not yet formally or officially in existence. Purely as an interesting exercise, ask yourself, as a reader, to determine if the subject in any of these examples was an EPrag or at least demonstrated an EPrag's tendencies in the context of the illustration. This is all history now, but revisiting these bits of our past with the proper perspective may help us appreciate what might need to be done in the present and future.

Example One—Confucius and His Aphorisms

This marvelous thinker, about whose life not much is known, lived around 500 BC. Although he is the only one in these examples to have been considered a philosopher, Confucius is not simply known for his endless searches for truth and other abstract notions. Indeed, he studied and discussed the concepts addressed by later philosophers, but most of his well-deserved fame derives from his numerous sayings—aphorisms—pertaining to behavior on a day-to-day basis. With Confucius, any evidence of EP is not so much in his actions as in his writings and teachings, wherein he advises others how to pragmatically achieve desired goals. Although the following are not project specific, they are worthy of consideration for general application:

With regard to governing, three quotes follow:

1. He who exercises government by means of his virtue may be compared to the north polar star which keeps its place while all other stars turn toward it.

2. Do not be desirous of having things done quickly for the sake of getting small benefits. This usually prevents things being done thoroughly and focusing on small benefits prevents big things from being done at all.

3. If language is not correct, then what is said is not what is meant; if what is said is not what is meant, then what must be done remains undone; if this remains undone, morals and art will deteriorate; if justice goes astray, the people will stand about in helpless confusion. Hence, there must be no arbitrariness in what is said as this matters above everything.

And a few more quotes about pragmatic attitudes and actions in life follow:

1. A person who has committed a mistake and doesn't correct it is committing another mistake.
2. Before embarking on a journey of revenge, dig two graves.
3. To move a mountain, one begins by carrying away small stones.
4. Our greatest glory is not in never failing, but in getting up every time we do.

Example 2—Charlemagne (AD 742–814) and His Expediency

Charlemagne is known principally as head of what has come to be known as the Holy Roman Empire. But before being crowned by Pope Leo III as an emperor (AD 800), he had governed effectively for over thirty years. During that time his pragmatic actions to establish order in government, trade, and society in general had great and lasting influences over the future of Europe. Unfortunately, not long after his death, much of what he had worked to attain became corrupted or was abandoned out of ignorance, thus delaying the development of Western civilization for centuries.

The following are four simple examples of his pragmatism:

1. **Early champion of unification.** Charlemagne was a great warrior, tactician, and commander of men. These attributes in others have produced leaders who were nothing more than conquerors. Charlemagne's military actions, however, appear to have always been for a particularly useful (and pragmatic) political purpose, such as the rescuing of peoples and cultures in regions from Iberia to Rome. Combined with his administrative skills, Charlemagne's military victories resulted in his crafting the first unification of Western Europe.

2. **Tolerance toward the Jews.** After his coronation and not long before his death, Charlemagne enacted the Capitulary for the Jews, a series of laws restricting Jewish activity in the empire. There is some controversy as to why this was done and whether the restrictions were enforced by Charlemagne even in the brief time remaining in his life. The reason for this law is somewhat of a mystery, because Charlemagne, by his actions, had always ignored the church's anti-Jewish pronouncements, policies, and dogmas in order to give Jews protection, freedom, and opportunity to thrive in his domain. Being a pragmatist, he also knew it would serve him and his realm well, because he believed, with justification as history has shown, that the Jewish presence would aid the establishment of trade, facilitate commerce, and promote the values of education and enlightenment. Charlemagne seems to have surrounded himself with Jews whenever possible. His own personal physician and chief

diplomat were Jews, and he caused many letters to be written inviting Jews from everywhere to settle in his kingdom.

3. **Monetary and economic order.** Charlemagne was concerned with the economic future of his realm and that of Europe in general. In pursuit of that goal, he pragmatically abolished the chaotic ancient monetary system based on gold, which was in short supply at that time. He replaced the system with one based on silver, actually a monetary unit based on one *pound* of silver, the origin of the modern "pound" and other currencies. He then enacted the Capitulare de Villis, a set of rules and standards establishing an early guide for accounting practices, including an organized method of detailing and preserving information about income and expense records, thus bringing order to trade.

4. **Fostering education and enlightenment.** In Charlemagne's time, very few people were literate, let alone educated. Charlemagne himself was illiterate for most of his life, as were substantially all monarchs for some time to come. Nevertheless, recognizing the value of learning and knowledge, he was able to produce an era that flourished with scholarship, science, art, and literature. He reached out to every culture with which he was in contact and sought to bring to his court learned peoples from wherever they could be found. So much were his achievements in this area that today many refer to the period as the Carolingian Renaissance.

Example 3—Elizabeth I of England (1533–1603) and the 1558–59 (second) Act of Supremacy and Act of Uniformity

When she ascended the throne, the young Elizabeth found herself in the midst of a potential civil war between Protestants and Catholics. In a bold move reminiscent of her father but for more pragmatic reasons, after arranging parliamentary compliance (Second Act of Supremacy), she declared herself supreme governor of the Church of England and instituted an Oath of Supremacy. This required anyone taking public or church office to swear allegiance to the monarch as leader of the church and state. Anyone refusing to take the oath could be charged with treason.

Her pragmatic choice of the term supreme governor, as opposed to supreme head, pacified both Catholics and Protestants. Both factions, for spiritual and sociopolitical reasons, could not abide a woman rivaling the pope or the archbishop of Canterbury by being called the "head" of anything religious.

She followed the Act of Supremacy with the Act of Uniformity, which required subjects to attend the same church. This church fused the customs and rituals of Catholicism and Protestantism and allowed worship in either the Catholic or Protestant manner. Elizabeth, who was not religious and could not have cared less about favoring either Protestants or Catholics, was a *politique,* a term then used for someone in authority placing the interests of the country above other concerns. She did not prosecute anyone for religious actions unless those actions directly undermined the authority of the English crown.

These pragmatic measures officially established the Anglican Church in England. In the manner she chose, she was able to avert the catastrophe of religious war. By implementing both acts, she unified the country. This set the stage for the Elizabethan era, a glorious period in English history.

Example 4—William Shakespeare (1564–1616) and His Verses

Similar to the situation with Confucius, Shakespeare's actions are not the issue, but rather the things his verses tell us about how he thought and would have others act. In his most famous play (*Hamlet* I, iii, 55–81), Polonius's farewell advice to Laertes is replete with pragmatic (and wise) doctrines. Here are just a few:

1. "Give thy thoughts no tongue, Nor any unproportioned thought his act." This would now be stated as "Don't say just anything that comes into your head" and "Don't run off half-cocked."
2. "Those friends thou hast, and their adoption tried, Grapple them to thy soul with hoops of steel;" Today, we would say, "Cherish your friends, and be loyal to them."
3. "Beware of entrance to a quarrel, but being in, Bear't that the opposed may beware of thee." Today we would say, "Don't start trouble, but if trouble finds you, act in such a manner that it won't find you again" or "Always do your best."
4. "Give every man thy ear but few thy voice." We say, "You can learn more by listening than by talking."
5. "Take each man's censure, but reserve thy judgment." We would say, "Don't be so fast to criticize" and "Learn from your mistakes."

6. "Costly thy habit as thy purse can buy, But not express'd in fancy; rich, not gaudy; For the apparel oft proclaims the man." This is now known as "Dress for success" and "Clothes make the man."

7. "Neither a borrower or a lender be; For loan oft loses both itself and friend, And borrowing dulls the edge of husbandry." Shakespeare knew that lending was risky on multiple levels, as was the failure to live within one's means.

And finally, the greatest fatherly pragmatic advice—something that needs no explanation and is of most importance from an EP point of view—is "This above all: to thine ownself be true, And it must follow, as the night the day, Thou canst not then be false to any man."

Example 5—Abraham Lincoln (1809–65) and the Emancipation Proclamation

The great sixteenth president of the United States was no stranger to being practical. Historians regard him as having been an extremely canny politician. Faced with the outbreak of the Civil War at the beginning of his presidency, and leading a nation struggling to prevail in the early stages of the war, Lincoln exercised what might be considered a bit of ethical pragmatism when he issued the Emancipation Proclamation (the "EP" initials are coincidental). Contrary to wide belief, the action was not based on altruism, conscience, or a strong moral conviction about slavery, but on doing something that would, among other things, hurt the Confederacy and give the North an advantage. In a letter to Horace Greeley in August 1862 prior to issuing the proclamation, he wrote the following (from *The Collected Works of Abraham Lincoln*, edited by Roy P. Basler, Volume V, pp. 388–389):

> If there be those who would not save the Union, unless they could at the same time save slavery, I do not agree with them. If there be those who would not save the Union unless they could at the same time destroy slavery, I do not agree with them. My paramount object in this struggle is to save the Union, and is not either to save or to destroy slavery. If I could save the Union without freeing any slave I would do it, and if I could save it by freeing all the slaves I would do it; and if I could save it by freeing some and leaving others alone I would also do that. What I do about slavery, and the colored race, I do because I believe it helps to save the Union; and what I forbear, I forbear because I do not believe it would help to save the Union ... I have here stated my purpose according to my view of official duty; and I intend no modification of my oft-expressed personal wish that all men everywhere could be free.

What Lincoln did here certainly was pragmatic, but was it ethical? Since the basic tenet of EP is that human life has value, there may be some question as to whether his motives conformed to the philosophy.

Nevertheless, Lincoln's actions appear to have harmed no one except the declared enemy in a war and doubtless saved many lives by strengthening the Union's position. This ultimately resulted in ending the war, which stopped the loss of life and ended slavery as well.

Example 6—Theodore Roosevelt (1858–1919) and The Great White Fleet

In 1907, Theodore Roosevelt, having been president of the United States since 1901, contemplated how to capitalize on the newly enlarged and modernized navy that he, with congressional approval, had recently developed.

After the Spanish-American War, the United States acquired possessions in distant places—Puerto Rico, Guam, and the Philippines. Japan's navy had demolished the Russian fleet in 1905 and appeared to dominate the Pacific, including the area of two of the new US possessions.

Some in the United States, among them Roosevelt, had aspirations about the United States being a player on the global stage, but history had not yet provided the opportunity to display America's prowess. America had been entering into treaties, but no one knew if the world's opinion of its strength would make the treaties viable.

Roosevelt believed that if he sent a sparkling new fleet around the world, it would serve many useful purposes. The world at that time lacked the technology and communications capabilities we now casually accept as if we always had them. So, first, sending this great fleet would provide an opportunity to represent the United States in a good light and extend American goodwill all over the planet. Second, it would demonstrate that the United States had become a major military and sea power. Third, it would give Japan the message that the United States was able to send its fleet to distant places to protect its interests. And last, it would afford the navy the opportunity to test, modify, and improve the technology of the fleet and strengthen the performance of naval personnel.

Roosevelt's plan was to deploy sixteen battleships divided into two squadrons, along with various escorts. The hulls of the ships were painted gleaming white, indicating a peacetime navy. Unfortunately, Congress thwarted the president's grand scheme of global circumnavigation by refusing to appropriate the funds necessary to do it. Basically, they said, "*No!*"

Roosevelt, always a pragmatist, was speaking softly, but he wanted to show all the other nations that the United States was carrying his proverbial big stick. So this is what he did. He announced that since he had only about *half* the funds in the budget to do the job, he would order the fleet to sail *halfway* around the world! If Congress wanted to leave them there, that would be their decision, but if they wanted to bring them back home, they would have to appropriate the other half of the funds. Knowing that Roosevelt didn't bluff, Congress capitulated and appropriated the funds. The fleet sailed on December 16, 1907, and returned on February 22, 1909. The deployment was a great success. It accomplished everything Roosevelt had intended and more. Because of the beautifully painted hulls of the ships, the force came to be known as The Great White Fleet.

Example 7—Emmeline Pankhurst (1858–1928) and the Suffrage Campaign

This woman, an activist in the women's suffrage movement, may have demonstrated EP more by her tenacity alone than many EPrags have demonstrated by the boldest of actions. Although tenacity by itself, in some cases, can serve to bring about the desired goals, it is Emmeline's positive actions and deeds that are impressive. As stated by Marina Warner in "Emmeline Pankhurst—Time 100 People of the Century," *Time* (June 14, 1999), "She shaped an idea of women for our time; she shook society into a new pattern from which there could be no going back."

Pankhurst was born as Emmeline Goulden in England and was educated in France. She was born into a family that was highly political, so she came by, and took to, activism naturally. (She is not to be confused with another famous suffragette, *Emily* Davison, who, in 1913, while attending the running of the Epsom Derby, was killed when, as a protest, she threw herself under a racehorse owned by King George V.)

There are two impressive things Emmeline Pankhurst did that I am pointing out because they relate to applying the principles of EP. (Again, the "EP" initials are coincidental.) The first one is about her passion for her cause and the means she employed to achieve success. Prior to the death of Emily Davison, she had engaged in a series of violent protests and campaigns to draw attention to, and garner support for, her cause. Hunger strikes, stone throwing, window smashing, and arson brought frequent arrests and prison sentences for her and her colleagues. The following is a telling quotation: "Human life for us is sacred, but we say if any life is to be sacrificed it shall be ours; we won't do it ourselves, but we will put the enemy in the position where they will have to choose between giving us freedom or giving us death"– (Emmeline Pankhurst speech, *"Freedom or Death,"* 1913).

You will have to judge whether the violence was justified by measuring what it cost against the fact that the ultimate goal was finally achieved. Some decried her tactics, but most believed the awareness brought about by the tactics made it all happen. It is plausible to assume that without her efforts, as severe as they were, the granting of the right to vote for women would, at the least, not have occurred until much later.

At the outbreak of World War I, while the suffrage campaign was in full force, Emmeline Pankhurst did the second impressive thing related to EP. She announced a temporary "truce" in the women's suffrage movement. She thereafter devoted her energies and tactics, as well as enlisting the cooperation and support of her colleagues, to support the war effort. Considering that the menace of the kaiser and the "German peril" transcended the voting issue, she said that there would be no use in fighting for a vote if there would no longer be a country to vote in. This is a prime lesson in pragmatism and another justification of violence (war) to reach a goal—the saving of one's country.

Example 8—Winston Churchill (1874–1965) and the Bombing of Coventry

Early in World War II, the Allies found a way to decipher the code of the German military. For decades, history told us that Britain's wartime leader, Churchill, was given an advance warning of the bombing of the city of Coventry by the Luftwaffe, after which he had to choose one of two options: (1) warn Coventry and undoubtedly save many lives; or (2) say nothing, leaving the Nazi war machine ignorant of the Allies' advantage with the code. Churchill chose the latter and sacrificed Coventry so that the Allies could continue breaking the code without suspicion throughout the war until victory.

Historians now differ on whether Churchill knew specifically that Coventry was the target or if it was London. Although this is only one example of the same practice Churchill used innumerable times during the war, the point remains the same. The ultimate goal, winning the war and saving countless more lives, dictated his choices.

Example 9—Harry Truman (1884–1972) and the Attacks on Hiroshima and Nagasaki

When Franklin Roosevelt died in 1945, Vice President Truman had not yet been informed of the project to develop a nuclear bomb. Shortly after being sworn in as president, he was briefed about the Manhattan Project and the potential for destruction of this new "wonder weapon." Not very long after learning about what is now called the "atom bomb," President Truman was faced with making the decision to use it.

In August 1945, the war in Europe was over and the Allies, principally the United States, were moving closer to Japan in contemplation of invasion to stop the Japanese military colossus. Some estimated that it could cost as many as one million casualties to invade mainland Japan and suppress the fanatical Japanese. In addition, other damage and loss of life would continue to occur in all Japanese-held territories. Truman's two options were clear— to use the bomb or to continue fighting a conventional war. There were compelling reasons why he should refuse to use the first nuclear weapon in history, but doing so would allow death and destruction to continue until the Japanese were finally defeated at some unknown and perhaps distant time in the future. Authorizing the use of the atomic bomb would most likely kill two hundred thousand civilians in two targeted cities, Hiroshima and Nagasaki, but in all likelihood it would convince the emperor of Japan that unconditional surrender would be essential for Japan's survival. As history knows, Truman authorized the use of the bomb. Two cities were destroyed and the civilians were killed as projected. But the war ended.

Example 10—Mohandas Gandhi (1869–1948) and the Indian National Congress (INC)

Gandhi was born in India and studied law in England. He lived in South Africa for a time before returning to his native India in 1915. It was in South Africa that he first employed nonviolent civil disobedience as a means to achieve civil rights for the Indian population there.

Back in India, he confronted the issue of independence from the British, who had been ruling in one form or another since the seventeenth century. In more recent times, during the Victorian era and through what was called The Raj, Britain ruled and totally dominated all of India's existence. Early on, there had been attempts to end their rule but without success. These efforts usually resulted in the slaughter of Hindus and Muslims alike. Gandhi wanted to get the British out of India but feared repeating the folly of the past.

Although he experienced only limited success with nonviolent civil disobedience in South Africa, Gandhi became convinced that violence would only bring about killing and suffering for the Indian people without changing the social and political order in India. He therefore decided to implement his beliefs in peaceful noncooperation as opposed to violence. He began by organizing the masses to engage in protests against excessive taxes and discrimination.

Prior to Gandhi's arrival in India, the independence movement had been waged only by the upper classes, which sought principally to improve their commercial circumstances but had little regard for actual independence. Gandhi changed everything by transforming it to a mass movement. He became active in the Indian National Congress to such an extent that in the 1920s the INC officially adopted his policies of nonviolence and civil resistance. He worked against poverty, for women's rights, for religious and ethnic equality, and to establish democratic freedoms for all.

It was Gandhi's belief that it was more pragmatic to wear down the British than to pay the price that a war would bring. He was right. The British could not endure the difficulties his campaign caused. As an example, because of his protests and noncooperation activities, in 1930 and 1931 alone the British had the burden of arresting, and maintaining in prison, approximately 100,000 subjects. Although he himself was imprisoned many times throughout the struggle, Gandhi never ceased to continue his nonviolent campaign, a great effort that ultimately led to the success he sought for his people.

Example 11—Martin Luther King Jr. (1929–68) and Nonviolent Civil Disobedience

Martin Luther King Jr. (MLK) was the minister of the Ebenezer Baptist Church, which his grandfather, beginning in 1893, had built into a major Atlanta house of worship.

In addition to preaching to his congregation, MLK wanted to do much more in the field of human rights, particularly with regard to the institutional discrimination against African Americans. As a young man he read and studied various works relating to peaceful solutions, including Henry David Thoreau's essay "On Civil Disobedience," but he initially practiced conventional self-defense, even having guns in his household as a means of dealing with potential troublemakers. MLK, exhibiting qualities of pragmatism, had no unrealistic illusions about the value of firearms in the hands of an often unprotected minority. However, although he considered many other options that might have been justified in combating the oppression, MLK, after a considerable learning period, came to believe that the most pragmatic way to achieve his particular goals would be through the use of nonviolent civil action. He wrote, "As my sufferings mounted I soon realized that there were two ways in which I could respond to my situation—either to react with bitterness or seek to transform the suffering into a creative force. I decided to follow the latter course."

The transformation began when veteran African American civil rights activist Bayard Rustin became MLK's main advisor in the late 1950s. Rustin had studied the teachings of Mohandas Gandhi and used Gandhi's tactics himself with some success in the 1940s. MLK had initially known little about Gandhi and rarely used the term "nonviolence" during his early years of activism, but Rustin guided him by showing him the alternative of nonviolent resistance.

Inspired by reading about and discussing Gandhi's success with nonviolent activism, MLK sought support in the United States from the Quaker group the American Friends Service Committee, which also rejected violence. With the committee's help, MLK was able to go to India in 1959 to make an in-person study of Gandhi's legacy. The trip to India convinced him that nonviolent resistance was the only pragmatic way to succeed in leading America's struggle for civil rights. He adopted the pragmatic methods and put them to use at home. MLK's efforts were rewarded by the greatest civil rights reforms in American history. When he received the Nobel Peace Prize in 1964, he invoked some of Gandhi's nonviolent rhetoric, saying that his accomplishments in the American civil rights movement were the result of a struggle using only the weapons of truth, courage, and force of soul.

Chapter 9

Pragmatic for All?

In trying to please all, he had pleased none.

—Aesop, *Aesop's Fables*

What is pragmatic for one may not be pragmatic for all. When I say "all," I do not always mean the whole world. Remember, EP seeks to find a cause that, in the most efficient, practical manner, results in an effect providing the greatest good for the greatest number. Often, there are conflicting interests within groups, institutions, religions, governments, and nations. Once again, as was stated in part 1 of this book, identifying a goal (effect) can be difficult. Even after a goal is identified and then sought, there may not be agreement on the exact cause necessary to produce the desired effect (goal). The following are some examples of how EP might be applied in situations of inherent conflict.

Example 1—Monetary Policy

Interest Rates—(All numbers are approximate.) Assume that interest rates are comparatively high; let us say 8 percent per annum for a first mortgage. This would mean the buyer of a residential property would pay interest of $8,000 per year plus some principal for every $100,000 borrowed. At another time when rates were lower—in the range of 2 percent—the buyer would have been paying only $2,000 per year in interest for each $100,000 borrowed. This is a difference of $500 per month for each $100,000! Two hundred thousand dollars borrowed would be $1,000 per month, and so on. Assume further that those much higher monthly payments do actually preclude potential home buyers from buying.

Some of the consequences of high interest rates and people not affording to buy houses and apartments are as follows:

1. Sociological impact on families wanting to sell/move or wanting to buy/move
2. Dwindling demand for new housing, thus no construction
3. Loss of jobs in construction and related industries
4. Loss of business for related industries, such as building suppliers, movers, brokers, furniture sellers, etc.
5. Less disposable income for those having higher mortgage payments and its effect on the economy

What is pragmatic for those listed above?

A possible solution (cause) to bring about the effect (correcting the problems above) is obvious. It would be to lower interest rates. Although one might argue that lower interest rates often cause higher listing and sales prices, generally, lowering interest rates would make even those homes more affordable because of the lower monthly payments. Buyers would buy, sellers would sell, developers would build, and jobs would be created in the fields of construction and all related industries. Lowering interest rates could be very pragmatic. Is it a boon to the economy? To everyone? Let us see.

What is pragmatic for another group?

In the United States alone, an estimated 50 million people depend, to some extent, on fixed incomes. This is about 25 percent of the entire US population. If interest rates stayed at the higher level, someone on a fixed income who had amassed savings of, let us say, the same $200,000 referred to above as being borrowed, could have been receiving 8 percent return on their principal each year. This would amount to $16,000 annually or around $1,350 monthly. After the lowering of interest rates, they might only get $4,000 annually and would lose about $1,000 a month! This segment of the population would do much better if interest rates remained the same or were made even higher. In example 1, lowering interest rates helped some and hurt some. Where is the greater good?

Example 2—Cancer Research

Cancer is ubiquitous. There is scarcely a person in the world untouched by the misery caused by cancer in some direct or indirect way. Curing and/or preventing cancer is one part of the quest for justice I describe in chapter 11.

Scientists, physicians, and technicians of all kinds and in every variety of institution are seeking ways to neutralize or eliminate this horrible condition. There is research around the globe. Studies and experiments are being conducted in laboratories everywhere. There are reports in medical and scientific journals. All this has led to great technological advancement thus far, but much more progress is needed. For those afflicted, time is crucial. An effective treatment available next year will not do anything for someone dying this year.

Currently, research and development take considerable resources and considerable time. Once a potential remedy of any kind is indicated— whether for prevention, treatment, or cure—clinical trials and studies commence. The research can take decades. Experimentation can take decades. Even after development, some studies can last for ten years or more. It all takes time.

As EP weighs in on this challenge, one pragmatic approach to consider would be helping to find a cure for cancer by encouraging researchers around the world to contribute to a universal database for sharing the fruits of their work *as they progress* rather than waiting until they publish a study. This would allow others to utilize what has been already done or learned, some of which might even be relevant to their own efforts. The result would almost surely lead to faster breakthroughs to treat and cure cancer.

It would not, however, be pragmatic if implementing the above process would eliminate the financial motivation of commercial interests or the desires of some to be acknowledged for their work. Much of the advancement in science is accomplished by the legitimate quest for financial success. In recognizing the various interests (whether commercial or academic) participating in any endeavor in this field, this proposition would require some method of appropriately crediting those making any contribution and protecting all commercial applications as well. It could be done.

This proposition in its basic form might be beneficial to most of the world, but unfortunately, as is indicated above, it might not be pragmatic for the pharmaceutical industry in particular. A great deal of research material is closely guarded rather than shared to ensure that the proprietor of the project reaps the enormous profits to be gained from a winning technique or product. Unless these profits could be guaranteed in some way, this would not be pragmatic for the industry, and it ultimately might not be pragmatic for the world. So going only partway with a good idea might defeat its purpose, whereas finding a way to afford the necessary protections to the interested parties might resolve the conflict.

Example 3—Labor Union Activities

Consider a contemporary labor-management relationship in the United States. For whatever reason, let us assume the workers are unhappy. For this exercise, we will choose the most common grievance: a desire for higher wages and/or more benefits.

There are potentially several courses of action to be taken by labor.

What is pragmatic for the union leadership?

The union boss may foster a strike because (1) his union members are disgruntled and he wishes not to continue receiving criticism; (2) he can demonstrate his own power to the world by ordering a strike; (3) he can wield power in withholding a resolution of the conflict, thus causing pain to the employer/industry/nation; (4) he can wield power in settling the strike and possibly receive benefits from both sides of the dispute; (5) he can justify his own salary/benefits; and (6) he can solidify his position in the union for the future.

In this case the strike yields benefits to the union boss, so it may be pragmatic for him to favor a strike. It may not be beneficial to the members.

What is pragmatic for the members?

Example: The members realize (1) if they strike, they will lose wages/ earnings during the strike period; (2) they risk losing their jobs as a result of closing the business of the employer if demands cannot be met and the employer decides to shut down the workplace; (3) they can ultimately lose their jobs if, as a result of onerous terms to the employer/industry, business functions are performed abroad; and (4) if they negotiate reasonably and accept a compromise settlement, they will continue to work and have a better chance of having jobs in the future.

What is pragmatic for management?

Sometimes the employer may feel that acquiescence to labor's demands is pragmatic because (1) an interruption in production as a result of a strike will be very costly in terms of lost product sales as well as market share to be taken by competitors; (2) bad publicity from a strike will harm the employer's image, resulting in lost future sales; and (3) the additional costs associated with meeting labor's demands will simply be passed on to the public.

What is pragmatic for the nation?

The nation may suffer from either a strike or the employer's acquiescence to labor's demands. In the case of a strike, depending on the industry, the nation could be affected by anything from inconvenience to a threat to national security. In the case of acquiescence, consumers would be paying more for the goods or services relating to the industries involved.

What could legislatures do to serve the nation? They could contemplate regulating strikes. If they are not corrupted by the influence of particular interests, they might act to inhibit or prohibit strikes as being harmful to the overall economy, the nation's population, and ultimately the union members as well. They may determine that a greater gain to a greater number is served by the absence of strikes.

Example 4—Populist Government Policies

Suppose there are two subjects—Subject Victim (V) and Subject Thief (T). Suppose that V works hard, follows the rules and laws, is a good parent, is an asset to his community, and has sufficient earnings and savings to be described as successful. He has money. Along comes T. T does not want to work. T is lazy, disrespectful, and slovenly. T does not have money. He generally disregards the rules and laws and has nothing positive to his credit. If necessary, he would commit a crime to get money. T needs money, so T draws the conclusion that since V has money and T does not, T should simply steal V's money … and, in fact, he does.

This appears to be pragmatic for T, the thief. He wants money and V has it, so T takes it and now T has money. Problem solved for T? Well, not just yet.

This was not a good outcome for V. He earned the money that T stole, so what appears to be pragmatic for T didn't work out very well for V.

Now let us change one fact in the above narrative. Let us assume that the government passes a law that allows everyone, including T, who wants money, to take money from V or anyone else if it is wanted, without calling it stealing and without it being a crime. Once again, it may be pragmatic for the T's, but it is not pragmatic for the V's.

Returning to the first scenario, in which T committed a crime to get V's money, let's see if this was really pragmatic for T. T could go to jail—not very pragmatic. Since he stole the money, T has done nothing to change his life that will make him more able to get money, so once the money he stole from V is spent, he will have to steal again if he wants more money. The next time V might be ready for T and might even physically harm T. Harming T might be pragmatic for V perhaps, but not pragmatic for T.

In the second scenario, T is not committing a crime by taking V's money, but are T's problems solved by taking V's money? I don't think so.

As you have already surmised, we are talking about what is known as government-sponsored "redistribution of wealth." This is a term about which EP would be very skeptical. The Merriam-Webster Dictionary (*Merriam-Webster.com.2015*) defines wealth as "a large amount of money and possessions." In my view this term is a calculated misnomer designed to ease the garnering of political support for controversial government policies. A better term for this would be redistribution of assets, since the Merriam-Webster defines assets as "something that is owned by a person, company, etc." In the United States, all but a few taxpayers really have "wealth." The V's in the United States are ordinary hardworking families and individuals who have limited assets from whom the T's take what they want. However, even the word *redistribution* is poorly selected. It implies that the "wealth" was initially "distributed," as, for example, to the wrong recipients. A more accurate term for this type of government policy would be "transfer of assets." Whatever the government policies are called, they authorize the taking of the V assets and the giving of them to T.

Similar to the outcome in the first scenario (thief steals from victim), in the government-sanctioned second scenario, T is still no more able to get money for himself without "stealing" it from V, leaving the T's with nothing but a dependence on what can be "stolen" from the V's. But worse than that, the V's might move far away from the T's (literally or figuratively) or be faced with losing what they have worked so hard to get. Without enumerating all the supporting policies of the so-called wealth redistribution, an objective and impartial observation clearly shows that these policies may be pragmatic for some in the short term but ultimately not pragmatic at all for most of society. They cause inflation, national debt, loss of job opportunities, and general harm to the economy, which in turn harms everyone. This, of course, is an obvious reference to all the failed socialist/communist policies undertaken in the former Soviet Union, Cuba, Venezuela, and yes, even in Communist China, which is moving jet-propelled away from those policies into capitalism.

Once again, the purpose of this example is not to favor a particular political belief, but to demonstrate the necessity of real assessment of facts and to impartially view the causes and effects involved.

Conclusion to Chapter 9 exercise

I repeat the caution about issues. EP does not favor or disapprove of any political or ideological positions.

In example 1, on interest rates, EP is neutral as to government intervention through monetary policy or free-market economy.

In example 2, on cancer research, EP recognizes that the contributions made to the health sciences by industry motivated by monetary gain could become nonexistent without careful consideration of industry's proprietary needs.

In example 3, on labor-management, the "society as a whole" may not necessarily mean the entire world, the nation, or even the industry. It may be confined to a smaller part of the overall society, such as all the members of that particular union.

In example 4, government policies not based on EP objective analyses and relying instead on ideologies, even if ostensibly benefiting one group in the short term, may in fact ultimately work to benefit no one and lead to ruin.

Thus EP is interested only in crafting the causes that produce the effects desired by the appropriate participants, because, in the context of civilization, pragmatism must be applied to the society as a whole, where the greatest good is afforded to the greatest number.

Chapter 10

Religion

How does EP reconcile the concept of religion with the philosophy?

> This is my simple religion. There is no need for temples; no need for complicated philosophy. Our own brain, our own heart is our temple; the philosophy is kindness.
>
> —Dalai Lama

> Religion is part of the human make-up. It's also part of our cultural and intellectual history. Religion was our first attempt at literature, the texts, our first attempt at cosmology, making sense of where we are in the universe, our first attempt at health care, believing in faith healing, our first attempt at philosophy.
>
> —Christopher Hitchens

> However many holy words you read, however many you speak, what good will they do you if you do not act on them?
>
> —Buddha

Many philosophies reject religion; many people do as well. Some people believe they are intellectually superior when they espouse atheism or agnosticism. Perhaps in many ways those people are superior, but religion is practiced around the globe by almost the entire world's population, including those acknowledged to have considerable intellect. There are also many theists who do not identify with a specific, codified way of following their own beliefs. Hasty dismissal of religion may not be justified for a number of reasons, the least of which is that the billions of followers of religious beliefs cannot be ignored. It is not pragmatic to ignore religion.

Thus, without making a theological evaluation, I conclude that there is a place for religion in the ethical pragmatist's world. Nor is it necessary to invoke the ancient aphorism about religion being the opiate of the masses. Religion as practiced in most contemporary civilizations can serve many purposes; for example, giving comfort to those who cannot be otherwise distracted when facing the blunt realities of life, providing a disincentive for antisocial behavior, satisfying the need to have a sense of belonging, and others. Recognition of these practices is essential to the formulation of any type of pragmatic perspective.

The major religions of the world (Buddhism, Hinduism, Islam, Catholicism, other forms of Christianity, Shintoism, Judaism, and numerous others in various cultures and places) consider human life sacred. Historically, few religions have not valued human life, although many have espoused human life values but acted in ways inimical to them. Some, by actual belief or simply by practice, have placed human life on the level of, or inferior to, that of lower animals. Examples are found among primitive unenlightened peoples and pre-monotheistic cultures that engaged regularly in human sacrifice. Other more recent examples are the Spanish Inquisition, ironically conducted in the name of religion, and the nineteenth-century resurgence of the Thugs of India, who worshipped a deity requiring murder. EP does not embrace or condone any cult, ideology, so-called "religion," or perverted form of any legitimate religion that countenances murder. (See addendum to this chapter for an article written by the author in 2002.)

When the populace of a culture becomes literate and develops a modicum of sophistication, traditional responses to many of the questions posed to religious leaders by their followers simply are not adequate. Logic, science, and experience demand something credible. Faith is simply not a sufficient answer for many. In modern times it is easy to conclude that organized religions are not discharging their obligations adequately. Many followers have abandoned their institutions and their previously held beliefs. Even those who ostensibly comply with religious doctrine frequently do so in form only and do not follow the tenets of the religion they claim to embrace. Our prisons are filled with individuals claiming to be followers of some religion. In the vast population outside of prisons, many of these supposedly religious subjects cause daily suffering around the world from their actions, some of which are ironically claimed to be in the name of religion. Today, the challenge of organized religion does not seem to be control of its followers as much as simply getting the followers to actually *practice* the teachings of the religion.

Although the ethical pragmatist is neutral regarding the beliefs of others, whether characterized as religion or not, there are lessons to be learned from applying EP concepts to even such notions as faith. These lessons may require an adjustment in the thinking of those responsible for the dogma of their respective religious institutions.

Although I do not write from the perspective of a theist, I have often pondered some of the questions commonly proliferated by believers for which there were inadequate answers. In the next chapter, on justice, I give illustrations of nonconventional types of justice. One example is the situation in which a loved one is tragically lost. I knew a young man whose mother prematurely died from cancer. The son asked his clergyman why his mother, a religious and exemplary individual, was taken so young. Why did God permit such an injustice? The response was something akin to "It was God's will." This is basically a non-answer. The young man, embittered by the tragedy and receiving no solace from his religion, left it. I asked myself what I could have said to comfort him had I been in the appropriate position. After considerable thought and respectful deference to the teachings of that religious institution, I placed myself in the mind of a theist. Then I analyzed the situation and concluded thus:

All living creatures inhabit a world that is filled with incidents of misery and suffering. Look around. The animal kingdom is rife with what we, as humans, would consider injustice. A lion attacks, kills, and eats a graceful young antelope that committed no act against the lion. We accept this as nature's way. People are born with, develop, or contract afflictions, diseases, and illnesses without being at fault. Do you remember the scourge of polio (infantile paralysis)? Volcanoes erupt; oceans and rivers flood; typhoons, hurricanes, and tornados blow; earthquakes shake; fires burn; and other natural and unnatural disasters kill thousands without provocation by the victims. There is no quid pro quo. They are simply victims. By any logical analysis this could not happen if there were the benevolent, protective God most religions claim to follow.

If God permits all this injustice, how can the belief in his existence be supported? Based on a pragmatic analysis, the answer is this: *God did not create justice.* Instead, God created man so that man could create justice. That is why man is distinguishable from all other living things. Other living things are not challenged to create justice or abide by it. It is a concept peculiar to man alone. And what is justice? Justice is not confined to what happens in a legal system. It embodies all that is right and should be right in a world that God wants man to develop, nurture, improve, and preserve. God meant for man to create justice through medical science discoveries and advancements to cure the sick, with methods to avoid conflicts and wars, by finding ways of neutralizing the impact of natural disasters, and in seeking and achieving all the goals envisioned in a utopian society. In the relatively few years man has been in existence, much has been done in terms of attempting to achieve this broad concept of justice, although it is obvious that considerably much more remains to be accomplished.

Earlier in this chapter I stated that there is a place for religion in EP. This is true, but in stating that, I was also implying what I now add—that the practices and actions of followers of their respective religions must be consistent with the teachings of EP. This does not mean that any of the followers need to abandon their faith or cease to worship as they choose *within the confines of their own religious domain.* It means that these worshippers must understand and accept that the entire world does not think or worship alike. This is critical to coexistence with EP.

The faith in religion may remain constant, but the ways followers of a particular religion act in society must take a secondary position to what provides the greatest good to the greatest number. For example, followers of a pacifist religion cannot cause a secular government to disarm or abandon the need to prepare for, and fight, a defensive war. Similarly, no religion should be able to impose its beliefs on an unwilling public. Any religions or followers that seek to punish or persecute nonbelievers do not belong in the EP community.

Millions of deaths and many wars have been caused by practices in the name of religion. It is not pragmatic to allow these practices to remain. The day of "kill the infidel" must be made to live only in the past. The practitioners of such antihuman beliefs must be eradicated like the scourge they really are. In practicing one's religion and in treating others who practice theirs, there must always be the requirements of tolerance, sensitivity, and consideration for others, but when any religion engages the rest of the world, the ultimate decisions to be made for all can be governed only by pragmatism.

Addendum to Chapter 10

Taking a Stand against the Thugs

E. Dennis Brod

(This article was written following the September 11, 2001, attacks in the United States at the time of the US Afghanistan incursion. Initially lacking universal cooperation, the United States was supported wholeheartedly by Great Britain.)

Three cheers for the British! Nearly a year after the September 11 catastrophe, America's great friend and ally is still supporting the war on terrorism. It's hard to believe that isn't the case with every civilized nation in the world, but there you have it. Why can't they all see what we see so clearly? That the only way we can ever be safe is to root out and completely eradicate these thugs. And make no mistake; the Islamic fundamentalist terrorists are the worst kind of thugs. By definition, a thug is a brutal ruffian or assassin. But the word has actual historic origins, and there are some striking parallels between twenty-first-century terrorists and the ancient "Thugs" who gave us the name.

The Thugs were ancient bands of assassins perpetrating their practices on the Indian subcontinent for centuries. Their beginnings are traced from seven Muslim tribes not far from Afghanistan as early as the twelfth or thirteenth century. By the nineteenth century, during the British Raj, they were practicing their cult of Thuggee by engaging in a perverted worship of the Hindu goddess Kali, the goddess of blood, disease, death, and destruction. Thugs, like today's terrorists, would often lead normal lives, disguising themselves as merchants or clerics and even acting in a friendly manner to their intended victims before striking. When they were ready to commit their murders with pathologically religious justification, they would rove the countryside in bands ranging from a few to several hundred. True followers of Islam and Hindu were appalled by their deeds and beliefs, but as modern terrorists find states to support them, so too did the ancient thugs find refuge and protection from local officials with whom they would often share the plunder gained while committing murder.

The thugs killed tens of thousands each year on the Indian subcontinent. They then expanded their terror to British subjects and institutions. Commencing an undertaking to fight them was difficult, but the British, the then governing power, finally began to deal with them. Lord William Bentinck, India's governor general in the 1830s, and his chief agent, Sir William Sleeman, led the campaign with cooperation from regional authorities. It was a very dirty business. The Thugs were well entrenched, assimilated, and hidden, not unlike what we find today in Afghanistan, Pakistan, and other regions around the world. Scouring the world for nests of these vipers is no less of a dirty business today. But perseverance will out. In India, after a period of almost seven years of mass arrests and executions, British tenacity finally stopped the Thugs. All told, between three and four thousand were imprisoned or hanged!

In those days Thugs killed their victims one or a few at a time. Today's technology makes it possible for even one terrorist to kill thousands or even millions in a single heinous act. Of course, precautions should be taken and security measures implemented at home, but it is obvious to anyone who really addresses the challenge, that the only effective way to win is by complete eradication of the terrorists and their support. The British knew it in the nineteenth century and did the necessary with success. Would that other nations join us with the same resolve. The task we face demands a great effort and would be aided immensely by something approaching a common citizenship. But even if others fail to join in, Britain and America will stand together for however long it takes to do the job. It won't be the first time our families have fought together to achieve a difficult but ultimate victory.

Chapter 11

Justice

Knowledge which is divorced from justice may be called cunning rather than wisdom.

—Marcus Tullius Cicero

It is hard to study philosophy or, for that matter, to read very much about any advanced culture throughout the ages—whether Western, African, Asian, or Middle Eastern—without coming in contact with the term or concept of justice in one form or another. The quest for understanding what justice means and upon what it is based is at the core of the essential questions challenging philosophers since they began asking about their own existence. Since the concept is so frequently addressed, I felt it was necessary to make a few comments about it, because my definition and application of the concept of justice are broader and more encompassing.

Some philosophers may disagree, but in my view, justice is a concept that was created by man in his earliest stages of becoming part of a civilization. Only humans are capable of such a notion, inasmuch as defining "justice" requires abstract thought combined with evaluation based on applied empirical observation. These are abilities not shared by any other living creatures or organisms.

Aside from the origin of the concept of justice, there is a great deal of material on defining justice and a huge variety of perspectives on it. The subject has been pondered, debated, and analyzed from the time of the ancient Greeks until the present. Plato had one of the broader interpretations, in which he gives great importance to justice, believing it includes the whole duty of man's behavior as it affects others. Thomas Aquinas felt that mere legal justice was not a sufficient human application. He believed that justice was required in all human relations (*Aquinas, Summa Theologica 2a2ae. 58.7*).

Some philosophers saw justice in terms of the theory of natural law, while others viewed it in the context of the social contract tradition or as being defined by the consequences of man's actions. The conclusions and comments are voluminous enough to provide a life's work for someone motivated in that area. Without making exhaustive reference to past works, I will simply observe that generally the thoughts about what identifies justice are considerably more restricted than mine.

For me, justice is not confined to a narrow set of definitions, but it includes all things in which fairness and the concept of right can apply. As I stated, most of the philosophers and writers who treat the subject of justice express their beliefs only in terms of what they call or indicate as political justice, while others expand the concept so that it extends to economic justice as well. (See the Notes at the conclusion of this chapter for a brief commentary on one aspect of justice in the legal sense—the role of government.)

In the political and economic areas, I have no doubt that perceived injustice is the motivator of much societal activity and a major contributor to violence. But as I said, for me the concept is greatly expanded beyond those categories, in which reaction is confined to alleged misdeeds of some humans against others. In order to bring true fairness to mankind, the kind of justice I envision must be sought and established in all realms— political, economic, social, and scientific. See chapter 10 ("Religion") for a more theological perspective of justice.

Traditionally, justice has been given many meanings, from the wise application and use of authority and power to everyday acts of the populace in simply upholding what is fair, right, appropriate, valid, or of sound reason. The Merriam-Webster Dictionary (*Merriam-Webster.com.2015*) states the secondary meaning of justice as conformity to truth, fact, or reason. By contrast, the Britannica Concise Encyclopedia (*2006 Encyclopedia Britannica, Inc.)* which advances the narrow conventional definition, relates that, in philosophy, justice is the concept of a proper proportion between a person's deserts, meaning that which is merited, and the good and bad things that befall or are allotted to him. It goes on to say the following:

> Aristotle's discussion of the virtue of justice has been the starting point for almost all Western accounts. For him, the key element of justice is treating like cases alike, an idea that has set later thinkers the task of working out which similarities (need, desert, talent) are relevant. Aristotle distinguishes between justice in the distribution of wealth or other goods (distributive justice) and justice in reparation, as, for example, in punishing someone for a wrong he has done (retributive justice). The notion of justice is also essential in that of the just state, a central concept in political philosophy.

My view, and the perspective of EP, is to seek justice in all of its aspects. This may mean supporting research to find a cure for cancer and other diseases and conditions; finding ways to increase safety on our highways and in our homes and places of work; developing technologies to improve agriculture, manufacturing, and communications; and addressing all human endeavors that can be improved in any way. EP does this through the recognition of reality, the analysis and evaluation of how to make improvements in a way that will work, and then taking action in order to attain the most benefit for mankind. Man has been seeking justice in this respect from the time before the wheel. Inventions, innovations, cures, and treatments all were the results of a search for a just remedy, solution, or effect. From Johannes Gutenberg to Jonas Salk and all those before, after, and in between who have striven to find a newer, better way to get something done, they have all been seeking justice for mankind.

For those who believe in a deity, I have stated that the supreme beings of known religions did not create justice. Justice as we have come to know it is elusive and is not encountered in nature. It appears only in those few instances when man has brought it into being. The compelling inference to be drawn from a theological analysis (covered in more detail in chapter 10) is that the Supreme Being (God) may have physically created the universe, the earth, and all things within it, including man, but justice was left for man to create. Stated another way as theists might, God created man so that man could create justice. Perhaps this is a test or experiment, but it is clear that unless man achieves justice, it does not occur.

Following the foregoing analysis, the justice that man was to create is meant in its widest sense. As has been stated, it certainly includes social, political, legal, and moral justice, but it also includes justice in the sciences and every other human endeavor, as was previously suggested. We have said that the conventional definition of justice equates it with what is fair and right. But as an illustration of the less recognized meaning of justice, consider the all too common situation visited in chapter 10 in which a loved one dies prematurely, perhaps in an automobile collision or from cancer. The consequential lament is often to question the existence of God by asking, "How could God permit this?" The answer is that God did not permit this; man did. The justice that God hoped for man to create in these circumstances would have been for man to provide methods to prevent the collision or develop ways to prevent or cure the cancer. In these instances, it does not seem "fair" or "right" that these people should have died—it was not just.

Perhaps the greatest reality I can offer about justice in any form is that justice does not simply occur. One can work for it and sometimes have to fight for it, but ultimately it is man that has to bring it into being. The search for justice involves devotion, vigilance, and often pain. Justice must be sought by all manner of effort and determination, including both constructive and destructive means, which may include anything from health-related research to war. When attained, it is man's greatest triumph. (See Notes.)

Notes to Chapter 11 ("Justice")

We tend to look to government for justice in the legal sense. This is understandable, since government has the principal machinery to provide it and presumably has the duty to provide it as well. But of all man's goals, both tangible and intangible, justice is the most elusive. If government should provide it and it is so elusive, then following closely behind government's priority to provide justice must be its obligation to at least instill a perception of justice, for justice not perceived might very well be justice that does not exist. As I have stated, perceived injustice is the motivator of much societal activity and a major contributor to violence.

Take the following view. Any advanced society in general, and its government in particular, would seem to have the responsibility to do everything necessary to eliminate ignorance and mental illness. Realistically, however, there will always be those who get a distorted picture of reality as a result of ignorance or their own infirmities. This means that government, even acting at its best, is incapable of communicating a sense of justice to the entire population. It follows then that government must communicate a sense of justice to mainstream society in all of its actions. This cannot be done simply by mouthing platitudes about fairness and equal treatment under the law. It must be done by behavioral examples of those in government and by application of the principles of justice in small things—things that the deserving citizenry encounter in their daily lives. As an illustration, a government's actions in appointing a staff of taxpayer-compensated lawyers to defend a career criminal in a capital case will not impress a citizen who is wrongfully required to pay a parking fine.

Charles Beard in his classic work about the US Constitution held that economics is the basic motivation for societal activity, but I believe that economics, although a powerful motivator to be sure, is not primary. The underlying and fundamental motivator, of which economics is the progeny, is basic human insecurity or, more accurately, the instinct to survive.

Injustice, or the mere absence of justice or its perception, threatens our survival. The typical citizen or dweller around the world does not seek political office or aspire to rule a nation. But consider the motivation of those who do. These subjects, coming from all levels of our huge and diverse populace, can become holders of public office or despots. To certain personalities among them, their perceived threats to security and survival are exaggerated. This is sometimes called paranoia or a tendency to catastrophize. Often this results in their quest for power as a result of fearing injustice and in the belief that power over others will keep them safe. Of course, it often does the opposite, as those in positions of power frequently come to lament. Fame itself as a means to power is often merely a magnified and distorted form of achieving economic security. Radical groups, revolutionaries, dictators, and other malcontents—some neurotic, some psychotic—are generally reacting to injustice, whether real or imagined. Does government have to assuage those who are in the extreme categories? I do not think so, but it must provide a level of justice that makes the general population feel that they are treated fairly.

Therefore, in terms of justice, both perceived and real, the task of government beyond its essential purposes is the formulation of a fair method of keeping order, protecting the innocent, and resolving controversies that can be implemented for, and communicated to, the bulk of the mainstream population.

Chapter 12

Judges

How does EP address the problem of incompetent judges?

> But let our strength be the law of justice: for that which is
> feeble, is found to be nothing worth. Love justice, you that are
> the judges of the earth.
>
> —King Solomon

First of all, in spite of its name, this chapter is not the seventh book of the
Old Testament, although there is considerable wisdom to be gained from
reading that work as well as the wisdom of Solomon quoted above.

Instead, I am dealing here with the role of judicial officers or jurists in a
modern society—those who participate in the administration of what is
called "justice" in one of its narrow senses, the legal sense. Courts, and
the judges that serve in them at all levels, provide a manner of resolving
conflicts, providing remedies for grievances, and dealing with societal
violations so that we can all avoid the alternative of violence.

These are the people who decide the fates of others in courts and other
tribunals all around the world. They do this by piloting the process by
which laws and rules are applied to conflicts and other matters requiring

some type of legal action. Thus a judge may be defined as any public official authorized or empowered to make rulings and render decisions or opinions in any process or proceeding within a general legal context.

Judges obtain their authority and are thus constituted as officials in a variety of ways in various cultures. In the United States there are also a number of different manners to determine how judges get to be judges. The two methods used in the United States are election and appointment. It should be said that many judges, whether elected or appointed, are honest and competent and do their job well, but the system we have in the United States is fraught with terrible possibilities that will be shown here. There is a volume of material on which method of choosing judges is better—election or appointment. Except to recognize the facts as they are, this chapter does not take sides in that debate, because the current EP conclusion is that both the basic methods with their respective variations are inherently corrupt and must be completely changed.

In the United States, some of the states and the federal government appoint judges. Most of the states elect their judges. Some judicial contests in the United States are actually partisan elections with judges running for office on a party ticket! Some states have a type of hybrid manner of selection sometimes referred to as "The Missouri Plan," usually with initial appointment followed by retention elections. At the appellate level most judges are appointed, even in election states. These appellate judges are generally chosen from judges who have been already sitting as judges at the trial level, usually for a considerable period of time. In that case there is more opportunity to determine how an appointed judge might perform in the new position. For illustration purposes, however, this chapter deals principally with trial-level judges, where the bulk of judicial activity occurs and where day-to-day justice is sought and is often absent.

Although the appointment process, for both appeals and trial judges, produces generally good results, there are still too many problems and there is a huge need for improvement. On the other hand, electing judges is a flat-out catastrophe. (See Notes to chapter 12 at the end of this chapter.)

Some reasons cited by experts against the election of judges are as follows:

1. Whoever spends the most money usually wins regardless of merit.
2. It allows buying judicial favors in advance and looking for payback in the future, making justice basically for sale.
3. It erodes public confidence in the court system, with people believing that judges are nothing more than rank politicians in robes.
4. When presiding over a case that may garner publicity, when the judge is not partial to one side or the other, particularly in an election year, a judge tends to make rulings and decisions based on popularity of issues rather than on merit or justice.
5. Voter participation is very low, allowing concerted special interests to easily buy the outcome of an election.
6. Incumbents have a great advantage, are rarely challenged, and are thus not accountable.

Just to cite a few examples about judicial selection from diverse cultures randomly selected, consider these:

In France, where being a judge is a lifelong civil service career, the emphasis is put on education. Potential judges must take competitive examinations that allow them to attend a national judiciary school (the ENM). (See *The French National School for the Judiciary*, Kelly Buchanan, Library of Congress, January 26, 2011.)

In Russia, the backgrounds and education of judicial candidates are scrutinized before the candidates are recommended to the president by a special qualifications board. The nominees of the president are then offered to the Federal Council for consideration and, ultimately, if qualified, are appointed.

In New Guinea, a similar process is used, with initial appointments for ten years. A national commission determines the rules and compensation applicable to judges.

Japan's court system is multitiered like the state and federal systems in the United States and many others nations, but without elections. The most numerous courts in Japan are at the trial level. They rely on appointment by special selection committees. The higher-court judges are appointed by various means in accordance with their constitution.

In South Africa all permanent judges are appointed by an elaborate process involving the nation's president, an impartial body called the Judicial Service Commission, and leaders in the South African National Assembly.

In observing the methods of selecting judges around the world, it is interesting to note that there seems to always be a process of vetting and qualifying the candidates to ensure their suitability. Except for the high-profile US Senate confirmation hearings regarding appointees to the US Supreme Court, very little attention is paid to the qualification of judges in the US, whether in state or federal courts and regardless of how they are chosen or elected.

In almost all of the cultures around the world, with the exception of the United States, the general public has little, if anything, to do with selecting judges. This is not antidemocratic; it is simply the recognition of reality (always required by EP)—that is, that the general public is not qualified to select judges. In the United States where judges are elected, only a notoriously small part of the electorate votes. They have little knowledge or understanding of the consequences of their votes and are essentially oblivious to the nature and seriousness of what transpires following the election, but they decide who serves.

If the system in the United States is so bad, you may well wonder why, if no one else, lawyers at the very least do not call for a change. There are good reasons why it is rare to find criticism from practicing lawyers about individual judges, or judges as a group. It is also rare to find criticism of the systems that put judges in their respective positions. In fact, comment of any kind, negative or positive, is difficult to find.

There are two reasons why even commenting about this subject is a problem. First, lawyers to some degree favor certain judges and wish to avoid others. It would not be prudent to be vocal in either of these circumstances, as it could suggest corruption in terms of the favorites and result in disasters such as bad rulings and decisions as to the nonfavorites. The second reason is that lawyers are generally prohibited by the rules of the bar (established, by the way, by the judges themselves) to ever disparage or make any negative comments about judges or the system of justice where they practice. So much for freedom of speech at the local level! Lawyers are reprimanded, fined, and even jailed for what most of us would consider fair comment. Unfortunately, most lawyers who run afoul of any of these rules, like one of the oft-used rules violations, "conduct prejudicial to the administration of justice," are loathe to take appeals. In the unusual event of appealing into the federal court system, they frequently are given relief on constitutional grounds, but those getting the relief are generally "tainted" thereafter.

Regulating lawyers for what they say about judges is usually justified by the need to maintain public confidence in the judiciary, noting that lawyers give up certain rights when they become members of the bar. Remember, bar rules are normally not made by legislatures, they are routinely made by judges.

The general opinion of lawyers around the United States regarding elected judges is that although there are some competent, impartial judges, many judges at the trial level are incompetent, corrupt, or both. This is a tragedy for fairness and justice, affecting all of society. Additionally, confidence in the judiciary can be maintained only by having a judiciary worthy of the public's confidence. When judges are competent, impartial, honest, and hardworking, they command and deserve respect and will receive it. One of the ironies about election of judges is that instead of getting the best from the body of available lawyers, the public often gets the worst because in many cases it is the unsuccessful lawyer who runs for the office of judge to get an improvement in income and benefits.

Regarding the restrictions on lawyers' comments, as an example, Rule 8.2(a) of the West Virginia Rules of Professional Conduct forbids a lawyer to make statements knowingly *or* recklessly that falsely impugn "the qualifications or integrity of a judge, adjudicatory officer or public legal officer." Rules 8.4(c) and (d) forbid dishonesty and conduct prejudicial to the administration of justice. What constitutes something that will "falsely impugn" is subject to a lot of interpretation, posing a risk in making any statement. Lawyers have no need for problems in addition to the practice of law itself, so it is not likely that they will engage in any kind of activity or rhetoric that will place them in the way of one of those catch-all rules.

Comparison of Judges to Super Bowl Officials

Athletic competition has been with man even before the Greeks organized the first Olympic games millennia ago. Today, sports competitions are a major part of world culture, attracting spectators and followers in the hundreds of millions and generating revenues that rival even the biggest of conventional industries. In the United States, consumers spent over *$25 billion* on professional sports alone in 2015 and this is without the gambling activity. Annual gambling in the United States is estimated to be nearly *$35 billion*. The worldwide figure for spending in sports and its related activities is believed to approach *$1 trillion!*

I am going to focus on only one event in all of world sports competitions to illustrate the nature and severity of corruption in the existing methods of constituting the judiciary in the United States. That event is the Super Bowl. This event has a sufficiently high profile and enough popularity to justify its being chosen as something to which most of us can relate.

To emphasize its significance, this competition 2016 was watched on television by an estimated 115 million viewers, the most-watched event in American television history. It is known to all Americans and most others around the civilized world as the final contest, of sixty minutes' duration, between two American-style football teams vying for the annual championship title awarded by the National Football League (NFL), an American private business enterprise.

Forbes magazine writer Kelly Phillips Erb found that for the 2015 Super Bowl, television advertisers spent an estimated $360 million just to air messages about their services and products during the broadcast of the game itself and the ancillary activities both preceding and following the game.

The amount of gambling on the Super Bowl can only be estimated, but with Americans wagering the approximately $35 billion that has been documented, it is certainly a massive amount.

A relatively new phenomenon in American football, particularly relating to the NFL, is fantasy football, a virtual sport that allows members of the public to "own" teams consisting of rosters that refer to real players. The players compete and perform in reality, and the results of their performances are applied to the virtual setting. In 1988, this leisure pastime counted approximately 500,000 participants; by 2015 the number had risen to over 41 million! As much as $5 billion annually is estimated to be generated by the activity through website, magazine, and television advertising sales, as well as league memberships and other commerce. This is in addition to the unknown amount wagered on weekly games and other fantasy contests plus the Super Bowl itself (FTSA.org, site of Fantasy Sports Trade Association).

Anyone gambling on any game, including the Super Bowl, which is the focus of this illustration, would certainly hope that corruption was no part of it. The winning team also benefits greatly from the victory, as do the players on the team and all those connected with it such as agents and product sponsors. Beyond the monetary aspects of the occurrences in, and outcome of, the game, the innumerable fans have a significant stake.

Based on the magnitude of participation and significance of the game, it is reasonable to assume that there is a vast reliance by every participant and spectator on completely unbiased officiating. The impact of officiating cannot be overstated. The "judges" in this relatively brief event were called upon approximately 150 times for their decisions in the last Super Bowl (*Krossover.com*).

Just think what chaos might ensue if the officials in the game were corrupt, biased, or incompetent!

The NFL, to its credit, engages in rigorous, meticulous procedures to select and maintain its officials at the highest level of integrity. This is how it is done:

Normally, an official begins by working in contests with considerably less interest and significance, such as at the secondary-school level. Only through years of experience honing their skills and through exposure to more and more scrutiny as the level at which they perform increases do they ultimately rise to a point where they acquire the competency and integrity demanded by the final post in the National Football League.

But even before being finally accepted as an official in the NFL, candidates must be psychologically screened and submit to, and pass, professionally administered psychological tests. They are also tested to ensure a thorough knowledge and complete grasp and command of the rules of the sport. Throughout their careers they have shown that they are beholden to no one except their employer—in this case, the league—which requires complete objectivity in enforcing the rules of the game.

Having made the point about the officials who qualify to be "judges" in the NFL, and specifically at the Super Bowl, keep in mind the importance of their honesty and ability to act fairly and objectively during the game. Now think about a comparison to other situations with two contestants. Instead of on the athletic field, the contest is in the courts, where the outcomes could affect the lives of the contestants much more than which team wins a football game.

Judges, particularly elected judges, can become judges without ever having set foot in a courtroom! There is no psychological screening, no psychological testing; there is no testing for knowledge of the law or for legal acumen. With very rare exceptions, in the US for trial-level judges in civil or criminal cases, whether elected or appointed, there is no requirement for experience in a lower court and no opportunity to observe or rate their impartiality or integrity.

Imagine if all the officials at the Super Bowl, including the videotape reviewers, were in place as a result of the same process of how we get our judges in the United States. If the NFL officials ("judges") ran for election, they could receive campaign contributions from the general public and from special interests as well. They might receive contributions from the teams that play before them in the games! Would the special interests that paid them be expecting something in return? If the NFL "judges" were appointed by persons other than the NFL itself, who would the appointers be? Perhaps a committee of some kind. Would the NFL "judges" be indebted to the people on the committee? What would motivate people on the committee? Would it be payback for past favors or an expectation of favorable rulings for their own interests in the future?

If you were interested in the Super Bowl, would you want the decisions being made on the field of play to be the responsibility of someone elected or appointed as described above? Certainly not. But what if you were appearing before a judge whose decisions in either a bench or jury trial were critical to your well-being or even your life? Would you want a judge chosen by these questionable methods? Well, this is what we have now and what you will be facing in almost every situation in which there is a possibility of one side of a matter being favored over the other.

It is sad to note that a private commercial enterprise (the NFL) screens, trains, and qualifies its judges (officials) with more diligence and scrutiny than our judicial system does, where its judges pass on matters as serious as life and death.

Remember, with all the superior training, testing, and scrutiny from this one private organization, the Super Bowl is still *only a game*! What should we be doing for ourselves in real life? Look at the following for an EP method.

EP would approach this situation with a pragmatic remedy to address the exposed shortcomings of the existing system. The suggested remedy might look something like this:

The Ideal Judge—A Career Professional

The potential jurist begins in law school. While in law school, the candidate applies for acceptance into a judicial school program (graduate degree). If accepted into the two-year program, the candidate attends school while working in paid jobs assigned to the candidate in the public sector. There would be three mandatory jobs: the first, clerking for a civil trial judge; the second, in criminal public defense; and the third, as a prosecutor. There would be mandatory completion of jury trials in the latter two areas. A committee/review board would monitor all progress during the program. If the program were completed satisfactorily, the new judge would receive an assignment as a judge in the lowest-level tribunal, such as a municipal or traffic court.

Throughout the tenure of the judge, conduct and performance would be constantly monitored and reviewed for competency, integrity, and demeanor.

The candidate acquires the title "judge" immediately upon the first appointment and retains the title until leaving the program. Sitting judges then move up in court levels as decided by the review board after meeting various criteria, such as number of trials, years of service, etc. Although he has earned the title "judge," the party cannot continue to be called judge unless he retires from the program pursuant to program rules and leaves the practice of law. A judge who retires or leaves the program for any other reason cannot retain the title in the practice of law.

Summary of Chapter 12

Judges are important to society for the maintenance of justice.

How judges are selected around the world is of importance to obtaining an impartial and competent judiciary.

In the United States, the system for the selection of judges is rife with the probability of corruption, bias, and incompetence.

A private commercial enterprise, the NFL, selects "judges" (officials) in a careful, prudent, and efficient manner to assure integrity and ability.

National, regional, or state governments, particularly in the United States, should develop systems to emplace judges who are qualified career professionals.

Notes to Chapter 12

(Recent item regarding judicial elections.)

In early 2015, the US Supreme Court issued a decision in a case involving a campaign for judicial office at the state level. One of the judicial candidates was charged by the state bar with violating a state judicial canon prohibiting those seeking judicial office from directly soliciting contributions to finance the candidate's election campaign.

Although campaign contributions to candidates for judicial positions are generally allowed, there are strict rules, laws, and guidelines as to how the contributions can be made. Usually, special committees headed by responsible individuals conduct all activities on behalf of the candidate. This is perhaps a fantasy about keeping the candidates impartial, as if they didn't know about the fundraising and its sources. But as bad as the campaign committee fiction may be, just think of what it would be like if potential judges were free to actually ask for money directly from lawyers and future litigants. Imagine the consequences of rejecting the request of a future judge and the possible level of intimidation associated with such a direct confrontation.

The candidate charged in this case used the First Amendment/free speech argument to justify the solicitation actions, and the case went from its local venue through the state Supreme Court and all the way up to the highest court in our nation. The state Supreme Court affirmed the actions of the state bar in finding the candidate guilty of the violation, and the US Supreme Court upheld the ruling as well.

When high courts are involved, the complexities of matters emerge. Concepts are examined, and positions clash. On its surface this case seems simple—was the act done or not? If done, shouldn't the case be over? After all, direct solicitation of money by a potential judge sounds like a rather bad idea. Well, believe it or not, the court was split five to four in the decision. Yes, four Supreme Court justices would have allowed the direct solicitation. The majority opinion, given by Chief Justice Roberts, supported the prohibition against solicitation, stating, "Judicial candidates have a First Amendment right to speak in support of their campaigns. States have a compelling interest in preserving public confidence in their judiciaries. When the State adopts a narrowly tailored restriction like the one at issue here, those principles do not conflict."

The total decision is an amalgamation of the majority opinion and both concurring and dissenting opinions. It takes a journey through some of the history regarding judicial campaigns and the rules pertaining to them. It discusses a number of related issues, like confidence in the courts, requests for recusal of judges who have received contributions from litigants or attorneys, and the plight of a judicial candidate without means who may be prevented from asking a close friend or relative for "a bit of financial help."

In this case, Justices Breyer, Ginsburg, Sotomayor, and Kagan voted with Justice Roberts in the majority, while Justices Kennedy, Scalia, Thomas, and Alito dissented on various grounds.

The issue in this case is worth knowing about for a number of reasons, as it shows many of the problems associated with election of judges. However, the Supreme Court, not being charged with rendering a decision as to allowing election of judges at all, avoided that issue.

My purpose in writing about this recent case is to demonstrate what EP would observe upon overviewing this affair—that election of judges is fraught with problems, problems that can be addressed by applying the principles of EP in the manner demonstrated in chapter 12.

Chapter 13

Capital Punishment

Can EP offer any guidance concerning the taking of a human life as punishment?

> Humankind differs from the animals only by a little, and most people throw that away.
>
> —Confucius

Notwithstanding the above quote from the huge body of wisdom left to us by Confucius, I am, once again, disclaiming the taking of sides in this ongoing debate.

The subject of capital punishment is treated differently around the world, but regardless of the universal applicability of much of what follows, for the purposes of illustration, I am specifically writing about capital punishment in the United States.

As a youth I was adamantly opposed to capital punishment, war, and violence of all kinds. Previous chapters have shown that EP became infused with the substance of my beliefs at some time after maturity and life experience became my teachers. One example is the justification of violence (war) when it is necessary to save lives. Irrespective of my own feelings in the past or now, EP approaches this subject without regard to the values espoused by contemporary moralists and ethicists or concern for religious attitudes and doctrines. EP does not care who supports capital punishment or who opposes it; its only concern is whether it works.

There are numerous arguments for and against the institutional killing of human beings, sometimes with formidable reasoning on both sides of each debate category. Some categories are the provisions of the US Constitution, morality, deterrence, retribution, the possibility of convicting an innocent defendant, discrimination against the poor and minorities, the administrative impact on the legal system, and simply the costs involved.

Historically, humans have been performing executions at least since recorded time. From tribal practices for one transgression or another and starting with the Code of Hammurabi almost four thousand years ago having numerous reasons for a death sentence, there have been crucifixions, inquisitions, stonings, decapitations, burnings, hangings, firing squads, and other creative ways of killing prisoners. Some methods are relatively unknown, and some, like the use of the guillotine in nineteenth-century France, are notorious.

This now brings us to modern-day America, where the first recorded execution in the New World was in 1608. Captain George Kendall of the Jamestown Colony in Virginia, having been convicted of spying for Spain, was shot by a military firing squad.

As of this writing, in the United States, thirty-two states allow capital punishment and eighteen do not. For the purposes of demonstrating ethical pragmatism in action, it is only for the states currently allowing it that some answer is sought for resolution or improvement. It is very difficult to get principled individuals to compromise their principles, so I am disclaiming once again: EP does not offer a compromise on this issue, but rather a method of dealing with the issue pragmatically in view of where in society this issue sits at the moment.

Why is a pragmatic solution needed? Consider the following (numbers are approximate):

1. From 1973 to 2013 (about forty years), in all of the United States, an average of 211 defendants were *sentenced* to death each year.
2. In the same forty years, there were approximately 27 *executions* per year on average—about 10 percent of death sentences.
3. Of the convicts awaiting execution (being on death row), the average time spent in prison while waiting, appealing to the courts, etc., is approximately 11.5 years!
4. A prisoner on death row (in current dollars) costs taxpayers an *additional* $90,000 per year to maintain than a non-death row inmate.
5. A well-regarded study in the State of Maryland found that just one death sentence alone costs $2 million more than a non-death penalty case. The study also found that for a total of only *five* recent executions the State of Maryland spent $186 million.

The answer to the question about why a solution is needed is that the entire capital punishment process is not very pragmatic. There is no credible demonstration of deterrence, but there is significant substantiation of the disproportionate and shocking costs. In capital cases, because a life is involved, the appeals process, even for the relatively few death sentences handed down, overwhelms the judicial process in general. Appeals courts and judges/justices are required to digest mountains of briefs, transcripts, and evidentiary material. All of these resources, costs, and efforts are presumably for the least-deserving members of our society (e.g., convicted murderers), while decent citizens are in many ways deprived of reasonable access to resolution of matters. This is the price we all pay to execute a mere twenty-seven felons per year out of a population of over 300 million! Is it really worth it? The answer is for the appropriate bodies to decide, but EP might approach the issue in a way similar to what is discussed below.

Remember that the following is not necessarily offered as a plan to be considered, but for the principal purpose of demonstrating how EP can be applied to a difficult, contentious reality. A plan like this could apply to all capital cases, or it could be modified to exclude, for example, terrorists.

Federal legislation applying to all the states would provide something like this:

1. States shall continue to decide as to allowing the punishment.
2. As to the states electing to allow the punishment, they shall be subject to the to-be-enacted "180-day rule," meaning that from the date of a sentencing of death, the state has 180 days to execute the subject. Thereafter, by operation of law, the sentence becomes a life sentence.
3. Following every sentencing of death, the state loses jurisdiction of the case completely; it then reverts to the federal system.
4. A special federal appeals panel shall be constituted to hear capital appeals only. Their review shall be expeditious and concluded within a fixed period; say, ninety days. Their decision is final except for a credible post-conviction discovery of new exculpating evidence.
5. In the event of the discovery of new evidence, a motion can be made only to one of the designated federal judicial panels that review such motions. The panel can order a stay only on strictly specified grounds and must decide within, say, ninety-six hours.

Pursuant to the above legislation, only a federal stay order can stop the execution. If no stay order is served upon the designated state official prior to the execution, the execution proceeds. If a stay order is issued and the 180 days pass without rescission or resolution, the death sentence is automatically converted to a sentence of life without parole.

The pragmatic approach involved in this example is meant to eliminate the emotionally and financially costly "death row syndrome," to free the courts for other matters, and to bring some form of closure to a painful situation.

Chapter 14

Immigration

Can we solve any immigration issues with EP?

> Give me your tired, your poor,
> Your huddled masses yearning to breathe free,
> The wretched refuse of your teeming shore.
> Send these, the homeless, tempest-tost to me,
> I lift my lamp beside the golden door!
>
> —Emma Lazarus

This chapter deals with immigration policy in the United States only to illustrate possible applications of EP for you, the reader. In the right circumstances, the principles of this philosophy might be applied to resolving the political conflict regarding immigration in general as well as the treatment of legal and illegal aliens, quotas, enforcement, and the like. But for the purposes of this book, the author is attempting to be completely neutral except as to peripheral matters that serve to help understand the philosophy.

The above excerpt from Emma Lazarus's sonnet *The New Colossus* was written for, and read at, the opening event of the Statue of Liberty in 1886; it was placed on a bronze plaque there later, in 1903. This work was not chosen to indicate a position on immigration. This beautiful piece of poetry was chosen because it expresses the sentiment that some Americans felt at that time. Many feel that way about immigration today. It is also quite interesting that the writer was not an immigrant herself. Emma Lazarus was born in the United States. Her ancestors came to America from Portugal in colonial times—before there was a United States of America.

Once again, the author specifically disclaims taking sides in this argument, for it will be the prerogative of the participants in government that ultimately decide US policy, whether in the legislature or in the courts.

This is a complex subject with many issues and sub issues, and although there is wide disagreement, for purposes of illustration, consider just three issues in the conflict. Other than individual beliefs and political strategies regarding immigration policy, the one area that can be more readily assessed is that of cost, so this chapter focuses on cost. Here are the three issues:

1. Preventing new illegal immigrants from entering the United States and/or deporting existing illegal immigrants.
2. Deciding the terms upon which illegal immigrants may remain.
3. Dealing with the costs of maintaining illegal immigrants in the United States.

Legal immigrants come to the United States from all over the world, as do illegal immigrants. They come from Canada, Ireland, Great Britain, Eastern Europe, Central and South America, the Indian subcontinent, Southeast Asia, Africa, Australia, Cuba, Haiti, and of course, from Mexico. Mexicans alone make up more than half of all illegal immigrants. Other countries of origin with a substantial presence are Guatemala, Honduras, the Philippines, India, and Korea.

In the following paragraphs, I will provide some general information and statistics (see Notes following chapter 14) to indicate the magnitude of the matter under consideration. Following the statistics, in light of the reality of numbers, how EP could approach the issue will be illustrated in terms of Mexican immigration.

First of all, many benefits and services are required to accommodate illegal immigration, some of which the general taxpaying public does not realize. These benefits and services relate to different categories, such as the following:

1. Direct benefits; for example, Social Security, Medicare, unemployment insurance, and workers' compensation insurance
2. Means-tested welfare benefits; for example, programs that provide food, cash, housing, health care, and medical services, like Medicaid, food stamps, and public housing
3. Public education
4. Population-based services; for example, public safety services—police and fire departments, streets and highways, and parks and recreation facilities

Estimates of the unauthorized (illegal immigrant) population of United States in the first decade of the twenty-first century range from a low of about 12 million to as much as 30 million!

In California, where it is believed the highest number of illegals reside, a conservative estimate of the cost for the illegals to every citizen who is the head of a household is around $2,400 per year. And this figure is based on the lowest estimate of the illegal immigrant population! Texas follows and has similar numbers, and the numbers everywhere are increasing. Georgia recently recorded the growth in its illegal immigrant population over a seven-year period to have been a whopping 152 percent!

In terms of demographics, it is important to note that immigrants in general, and illegal immigrants specifically, tend to be younger, meaning more children and a longer period of receiving benefits. Recent studies indicate that over 60 percent of illegal immigrants were ages twenty-five to forty-four years, and 53 percent were male.

There is conflicting information on the impact made by immigrants to the penal system. The Department of Homeland Security (DHS) estimates that immigrants (legal and illegal) comprise 20 percent of inmates in prisons and jails, with the foreign-born comprising 15.4 percent of the nation's adult population. On the other hand, the Federal Bureau of Prisons reports that 26.4 percent of inmates in federal prisons are non-US citizens and that noncitizens are 8.6 percent of the nation's adult population. However, federal prisons are not representative of prisons generally or of local jails either. Data compiled by other detention facilities report that non-US citizens made up over 10 percent of their total local jail population. Furthermore, Immigration and Customs Enforcement (ICE) in one period arrested more than eight thousand deportable alien members of more than seven hundred different gangs. Regardless of the conflicting numbers, the resulting costs for the administration of justice are estimated to be well over $10 billion annually.

It is a bit easier to gauge the number of illegal immigrants in the public schools where documentation is sought, but that leaves a great deal still unaccounted for. Education for the children of illegal aliens constitutes the single largest cost to taxpayers. The estimate for the children known to be illegal is approximately $52 billion annually, with most of those costs coming out of state and local budgets, adding to the burden of taxpayers at the nonfederal level.

Generally, it costs the public schools about $13,000 per pupil per year. This is paid for by taxpaying parents whose children theoretically receive a "free" public education, not to mention the parents who send their children to and pay for private schools because the public schools are so deficient. The Elementary and Secondary Education Act of 1965, Title I, was originally designed to provide supplemental educational funding in order to increase educational opportunities and improve academic performance of children from poor families. As one would expect, almost all children of illegal aliens meet the economic criteria of this program, impacting the program by about 10 percent and costing an estimated additional $1.3 billion annually.

Aside from the standard K-12 public school education, there is also a cost in the postsecondary area. Once again because of the economic status of most illegals, their children, whether born in the United States to illegal immigrants or not, meet the income qualifications for Pell Grants. The grants in this category amount to over $20 billion per year!

Regarding health care, some illegals have insurance from jobs, but most do not. Emergency services to all illegal immigrants are mandated by federal law; ER services alone count in the billions of dollars, in addition to the nonmandated but nevertheless delivered services amounting to many billions more.

Even the figures for border security and enforcement are substantial aside from the incalculable cost of the effort involved in the project. This, of course, diminishes attention to other areas of national security. The billions spent include costs for detaining and maintaining the criminal population, administration of deportation, general prosecutorial services, border fencing, and National Guard operations. According to the Congressional Budget Office, the cost involved in keeping *one* border agent in the field is nearly $200,000 annually.

Although it is difficult to calculate, illegal immigration costs US taxpayers about $140 billion a year at the federal, state, and local levels, with more than half the costs paid by state and local governments.

In addressing the three issues set out at the beginning of this chapter regarding immigration policy, let us consider the implementation of only one pragmatic law to make an impact on all three issues. The EPrag, in reviewing the current situation and in order to benefit from a cause and effect analysis, might suggest something like this:

The United States is a compassionate and humane country. We believe people should receive health care regardless of their financial ability and station in society. Likewise, we believe children, rich or poor, should receive an education. The new law will contain these provisions:

First, the United States establishes which benefits will be provided and then determines the conditions upon which those benefits can be granted to a *legal* immigrant.

Second, in order to receive health care or educational services, the subject must prove legality or be presumed illegal. *Illegals* will nevertheless receive the benefits. No one is turned down, but...

Third, if an illegal alien receives health or education benefits, *the United States will submit a bill to the country of origin for reimbursement of all services provided.* In this case it will bill Mexico.

Mexico is a trade partner of the United States. The United States must enforce collection of the costs of all benefits provided to citizens of Mexico by whatever means necessary. If there is no enforcement, nothing will work.

The projected outcome of the new law would presumably be the following:

1. Mexico will reimburse the United States billions of dollars in taxpayer monies spent on maintaining the illegals. The United States must employ the means necessary to collect these sums through trade sanctions or other economic and diplomatic actions.
2. The Mexican government, out of economic necessity and expediency, will put a halt to illegal emigration from Mexico to the United States.
3. The United States will have fewer illegal aliens in the future, and those remaining will not be costing the taxpayers anything.
4. The burden on immigration enforcement will be greatly reduced.

The foregoing might not make anyone on either side of these issues happy, but it is an example of how an EP approach could work. In this case it seems that it certainly could make improvements in a number of areas.

The hypothetical proposal was not tested in a laboratory, nor was it subjected to the kind of scrutiny that would be necessary if the proposal were actually being made to a legislative body. This is only a book, but this is an example of the type of remedy that can be developed by using a sensible approach to all matters—recognize the problem, identify the goal, and then craft a solution that will work consistent with the principles of the EP philosophy.

Notes to Chapter 14

The following are sources from which many of the statistics and facts in this chapter were taken:

Procon.org, "Demographics of Immigrants in the United States Legally: Countries of Origin, States of Residence, Age, Gender, and Jobs Held 2000–2012."

Federation for American Immigration Reform (FAIR) "2010 Report on the Fiscal Burden of Illegal Immigrants on United States Taxpayers," *http://www.fairus.org/site/DocServer/USCostStudy_2010.pdf?docID=4921.*

Association of Mature American Citizens (AMAC) website, "How Much Does Illegal Immigration Cost You?" Online article published February 27, 2015.

Congressional Budget Office Cost Estimate Report, S. 744, Border Security, Economic Opportunity, and Immigration Modernization Act, dated June 18, 2013.

Colorado Alliance for Immigration Reform (CAIRCO) website, "How Many Illegal Aliens Reside in the United States?"

Pew Research Center website, "5 Facts about Illegal Immigration in the U.S.," published November 18, 2014.

Department of Homeland Security, Office of Immigration Statistics Report, "Estimates of the Unauthorized Immigrant Population Residing in the United States: January 2012."

Immigration Policy Center Special Report, *The Myth of Immigrant Criminality and the Paradox of Assimilation: Incarceration Rates among Native and Foreign Born Men*, Spring 2007.

Center for Immigration Studies, study by Steven Camarota and Jessica Vaughan, "Immigration and Crime: Assessing a Conflicted Issue," November 2009.

Chapter 15

Noise

Can EP help in the problems caused by noise?

> Do not impose on others what you yourself do not desire.
> —Confucius

You may ask why a book espousing a philosophy would contain a chapter about noise. The author is using noise to serve as what one might call an object lesson. In urging the reader to use EP, it has been emphasized that making accurate observations is essential. Unfortunately, many of us are reluctant to do this in our daily lives for a variety of reasons. We may fear the truth. We do not want to be placed in a position requiring us to act. We do not like change. Often, because of convenience, laziness, or something as simple as personality traits, we accept our plight, suppress what our conscience tells us, and just live with it. So let us take this subject as an example.

It is remarkable how oblivious a substantial portion of a large population can be toward things that threaten them. The following are just a few:

1. Cigarette smoking
2. Using illicit drugs

3. Having unhealthy dietary practices
4. Engaging in unsafe sexual activity
5. Driving a motor vehicle after consuming alcohol
6. Recklessly operating a motor vehicle, like excessive speeding
7. Riding a motorcycle without a helmet
8. Carelessly walking, jogging or running on or near roadways
9. Cycling in obviously treacherous situations

There are countless other circumstances, places, and things that pose a danger or health hazard, but as was indicated previously, for one reason or another most people carry on as if they were invulnerable or completely ignorant. This behavior is confined neither to the young nor to any particular group of individuals. At one time or another, probably everybody does it.

This chapter's title reveals that this is about one of those seldom heeded, often ignored things: NOISE!!!

Had I not titled this chapter, "Noise," I might have dramatically announced the subject of the chapter with more impact *after* listing some of the conditions that noise has been demonstrated to cause. In any case, whenever it is read, I believe that simply reading the partial list that follows will make a significant impact on anyone concerned with one's well-being:

Noise can cause the following:

1. Ischemic heart disease
2. Coronary artery disease
3. Serious cardiovascular complications
4. Vasoconstriction
5. Hypertension
6. Immune system impairment
7. Birth defects
8. Impaired child development
9. Sleep disturbances
10. Tinnitus (ringing in the ears)
11. Hearing impairment

12. Stress
13. Increased workplace accident rates
14. Increased aggression among people
15. Numerous kinds of destructive antisocial behaviors

Without knowing the subject was noise, if any individual or group (including government bodies throughout the world, ranging from local boards to every parliament as well as the Congress of the United States or the United Nations) were told that by controlling *only one phenomenon* in our environment we could minimize or even prevent those conditions listed above, one would believe that they would surely respond with enthusiasm and a great interest in taking action. But it simply doesn't happen, even though some astute, caring souls have taken notice and admirably tried to make improvements. There are reasons nothing significant happens, but first let me examine what it is we are addressing.

What is noise? In common parlance it may simply be considered a loud or unpleasant sound. But it is much more, and it is quite bad. Unfortunately, it is seldom recognized for what harm it can do, both as an assault on our central nervous system and as the culprit in so many health and safety matters.

Some of those who have noticed the problems about noise have given the mass of these undesirable, excessively loud sounds a label. They call it "noise pollution." That name is an unfortunate choice. I consider that term to be a pollution of our language as well. Perhaps this is a result of the declining standards in the fields of reporting and journalism. In order for the phrase to have been comparable to similar phrases, such as air pollution and water pollution, it should have been called "sound pollution" or perhaps "auditory ambiance pollution" (a bit too much). But it wasn't, so we seem to be stuck with that name for now. Some more appropriately call it "noise disturbance." I prefer to use my own term, "noise intrusion," to define an unpleasant, unwanted, and unusually loud sound. The difference between "disturbance" and "intrusion" is that most people are aware of being "disturbed" by noise but are totally oblivious to the reality that the noise may be intruding on, and doing harm to, their central nervous system and other aspects of their health and well-being. This is enough terminology for now, but as is addressed in another chapter, it is important to recognize the significance of all aspects of language usage.

High noise levels adversely affect humans in all of the above-enumerated ways and more. Even our poor pets are victims. They can suffer ill health or actually die because of noise intrusion, which in animals tends to alter their instinctive predator or prey detection/avoidance capability, compromise their ability to navigate, interfere with reproduction, and impair their hearing.

Something seemingly unknown by parents of infants, toddlers, and youngsters is that noise is quite harmful to children in a variety of ways other than damaging their hearing. When you experience a baby crying or a child screaming or acting in a disturbing manner in a restaurant, it may be annoying and harmful to you, but it may be a lot worse for the child. Noise can cause actual pain to an undeveloped ear. It also produces an instinctive danger response—fear. This may be why the child is screaming or crying!

Most people are ignorant of the dangers of being in a loud environment and are harmed unknowingly. Adults are free to assess the harm done to themselves, but their pets and, of greater consequence, their children have no choice. They are both placed involuntarily in harm's way by their owners or parents.

In addition to the other health conditions mentioned in this chapter that apply to both children and adults, studies have shown that in school-aged children, even minimal sensorineural hearing loss has been associated with poor school performance as well as social and emotional dysfunction.

Normal sound rises to become noise when it interferes with normal activities such as sleeping, eating, working, relaxing, and conversing. Sound also becomes noise when it disrupts or diminishes one's quality of life. Some fundamentals of this problem are well covered in a US Environmental Protection Agency article by Catrice Jefferson, presumably through no fault of hers, employing the previously coined and ill-chosen label "Noise Pollution" as its title.

Chronic exposure to noise, even at lower levels, may cause noise-induced hearing loss and other conditions. Some people may be more vulnerable than others, depending on such factors as general health or age. As an example, older males exposed to occupational noise demonstrate more significantly reduced hearing sensitivity than younger workers.

High noise levels can contribute to cardiovascular effects. Exposure to only moderately high levels during one eight-hour period will often cause a statistical rise in blood pressure of five to ten points and an increase in stress and vasoconstriction. These responses lead to the chronic increased blood pressure (hypertension) noted above, as well as to increased incidence of coronary artery disease.

Furthermore, studies have shown that neighborhood noise, meaning noise from within one's household as well as noise from neighbors, can cause substantial anguish and harmful stress to residents due to the great deal of time people spend in their homes. Besides provoking quarrels and inducing rancor among neighbors, exposure can also result in physical symptoms such as migraine headaches and an increased risk of depression and many other serious psychological disorders.

Another important effect of noise is to make a person's speech harder to hear. The human brain compensates somewhat for background noise during speech production in a process called the Lombard effect, in which speech becomes louder with more distinct syllables. However, the Lombard effect cannot fully remove these background obstacles. Thus an attempted conversation made in a noisy environment frequently results in a lack of effective communication.

One of the reasons noise is so damaging is that it induces the production of cortisol, a steroid hormone. All humans have what science calls the "fight-or-flight response." Earlier in the history of human development, this response was activated by potential danger, such as the roar of a fierce animal, a clap of thunder, or a human scream. The response generated the secretion of cortisol, which, on a short-term basis, prepared us for action by raising our blood pressure and getting our heart pumping so that we were ready to defend ourselves by fighting or fleeing. Extra cortisol can work well when confined to infrequent and temporary situations. Unfortunately, continued extra cortisol is very harmful and we are getting it constantly because of noise. As has been stated by audiologist Professor Thomas Fay of the Columbia University College of Physicians and Surgeons, "Sound may no longer be an indication you're about to be someone's breakfast, but the vestiges of that long-ago time remain in the body."

Cortisol is responsible for many adverse health conditions, such as impaired cognitive performance, suppressed thyroid function, blood sugar imbalances (such as hyperglycemia), decreased bone density, decreased muscle tissue, higher blood pressure, lowered immunity, harmful inflammatory responses in the body, slowed wound healing, and increased abdominal fat. Abdominal fat itself is associated with a greater incidence of heart attacks, strokes, and other health problems, unlike fat deposited in other areas of the body. Noise-induced secretion of cortisol has also been linked to aggressive behavior, psychiatric symptoms, and increased rehospitalization rates. It can even increase symptoms of heartburn in patients with gastroesophageal reflux disorder.

The attitude of people toward noise is not unlike the attitude people used to have toward cigarette smoking (some still have the attitude). People could hear about the dangers of smoking, but while they were doing it they felt fine. So it is with noise. If you are at a concert, a noisy party, or in a loud restaurant, you may feel you are having a good time, but just like the smoke going into your lungs, the noise is penetrating your body, and there will be a future, and sometimes immediate, cost.

Sounds can be analyzed in many ways, such as to sharpness, roughness, and texture. Noise levels as well are measured in a number of ways, including frequency (hertz) and intensity. Here we will use the most commonly understood way to measure noise, and that is by its intensity. This is usually expressed in decibels (dB). The term was adopted to honor a pioneer in the study of sound, the last part of the term, "bel," being named for Alexander Graham Bell. The following illustrations relate only to decibels, the clearest way to comprehend the consequences of noise as determined by its intensity. Without using highly technical terms, a decibel is commonly understood to be a unit for expressing the relative intensity of sounds, generally on a scale from zero (hardly perceptible) right on up to the pain level and beyond.

To give an idea about decibels and their impact, one way of measuring the effect of noise is with the standard of permissible exposure time (PET). The charts for this are used principally to protect factory workers from hearing loss, but can apply anywhere, like at concerts, restaurants, sports arenas, etc. Noise at 85 dB has a PET of 8 hours. This means that one can be exposed to 85 dB for only eight hours before *permanent* hearing loss occurs. Note that this does not measure discomfort, interference with other activities, or the effect on the variety of health and social conditions previously mentioned. This is just for hearing.

As I wrote, for some people, noise may be damaging at even lower levels than 85 dB. For every increase of three decibels over 85 dB, the PET is halved. In other words, at 88 dB, you can tolerate only four hours without permanent damage; at 94 dB, you can tolerate only one hour; at 103 dB, only about seven minutes; and so on. A loud enough noise can, and frequently does, cause *immediate* permanent damage.

Generally, discomfort and possible harm begin at around 80 dB, with actual pain starting at around 130 dB. To keep perspective, I am listing some decibel readings at moderate range (the outdoor examples are usually experienced at a distance of at least seventy-five feet):

- 40 dB—average residence or small office
- 45 dB—level to awaken a sleeper
- 60 dB—normal conversation
- 70 dB—normal street noise
- 60–85 dB—most musical instruments and nonamplified bands
- 90–100 dB—truck without muffler; home lawn mower; leaf-blower; car horn

- 100–110 dB—fireworks display; wood saw
- 120–160 dB—amplified rock music
- 140 dB—artillery fire
- 180 dB—jet plane takeoff

Please note a little history. Artillery fire is shown above to measure 140 dB. In the First World War, a high percentage of combat veterans (some estimates are at 10 percent or even more) suffered with symptoms that included paralysis, amnesia, headaches, dizziness, tremors, tinnitus, hypersensitivity to noise, and loss of hearing. No brain or other physical injuries were observed in these patients. In spite of the trauma of war and the multitude of grotesque visions one can imagine these poor souls endured, the name given for this condition had nothing to do with fear, blood, or death. It was named after *noise*. The now infamous description/diagnosis of this condition was "shell shock." We now euphemistically refer to the psychological effects of war, including exposure to the noise of bursting artillery shells, bombs, and gunfire, as post-traumatic stress disorder (PTSD).

Because the effects in World War I were so bad, we may have suppressed our knowledge about the noise component after the war, leaving us with the ignorant state we are in today. We are all familiar with the term "peace and quiet." It is no coincidence that peace is linked with quiet, because there is not much peace in a noisy environment. Society frequently tends to ignore reality, as it is much more comfortable to engage in fantasies. That is why we talk about "peace and quiet" but never hear anything about "war and noise."

As a matter of interest about how we seem to ignore things that do us harm, I remind you that pursuant to the chart above, the decibel level of artillery fire and the noise that caused all the horrible damage to our servicemen is 140. According to *Sports Illustrated*, at a 2014 game in the home football stadium of the Kansas City Chiefs, fans set a Guinness World Record for having the loudest outdoor stadium by registering 142.2 decibels—more than artillery fire!

One of the difficulties in dealing with the noise intrusion problem is that most people and agencies who have addressed it at all seem to emphasize hearing loss with little regard for all the other ailments and conditions it causes. In the United States, the Occupational Safety and Health Administration (OSHA), for example, as well as the Centers for Disease Control and Prevention (CDC) have decibel standards for the workplace. Even allowing that the standards are acceptable, which is questionable, this is simply not enough to make a significant impact on the general population. Although the Environmental Protection Agency (EPA), prompted by the US Surgeon General's office, addressed this problem as long ago as 1974, its publication at that time was, and continues to be, ignored by all those who believe they have nothing to gain from acting on it. This is notwithstanding that the EPA set safe sound-level standards to prevent some of the disorders that noise was causing, including a number of personal disabilities, handicaps, increased accidents, behavioral changes, problems with concentration, fatigue, uncertainty, lack of self-confidence, irritation, misunderstandings, decreased working capacity, disturbed interpersonal relationships, and stress reactions. As to children, it has also found additional consequences of disruption of communication in classrooms and impaired academic performance.

Many of the noise intrusion problems affect only certain parts of the population—factory workers or those attending sporting events and concerts, for example. Other noise intrusion problems are more common and affect a larger segment of the population, as in restaurants, some retail stores, or other public places, particularly when music is sent out over loudspeakers.

Although excessively noisy music is onerous in general, one specific manner of delivering the noise is so bothersome that it rises to the level of abuse. This somewhat inexplicable phenomenon is the excessive use of electronic amplification, particularly for bass-range playing. I have named the applicable part of this phenomenon "gratuitous amplified percussion," or "GAP." It may indeed fill a gap in some of the listeners' heads. GAP is any amplified percussion sound that can be heard or felt by people other than the immediate intended audience. This is the worst part of loud music, because the pounding generated can still be heard and felt even when the music itself cannot be. If you are a distance from the music, you may hear the actual music faintly or not at all, but you will still hear and feel the pounding of the bass. If you are in a loud vocal environment like a bar or restaurant, the music may be drowned out by the voices or other ambient sounds, but the pounding continues. In some cases, whether you are a distance away from or actually at the "music" venue, GAP can sound like an aerial bombardment or a hyperactive construction site.

Some rays of hope have appeared in unlikely places. There are now a few restaurant reviewers around the United States who rate noise level as one of the factors in evaluating a restaurant. Some even do it in decibels, with many restaurants having noise levels of over 100 dB! Restaurants (including bars and lounges) are particularly culpable regarding noise. Building codes are generally strict about restaurant components, ventilation, occupancy, and other health and safety considerations but are, if you will excuse the term, *silent* about noise. And noise may be as dangerous and harmful as all the other negative conditions that the building codes are trying to prevent.

Generally, restaurants focus on visual aesthetics and totally ignore acoustics. Harmony, or what I call auditory aesthetics, is supportive of well-being and pleasure. In spite of this, customers continue to patronize excessively noisy places, ignorant of the real harm being done, even when they leave those places with a sore throat from speaking, an earache, or a headache. Some believe patrons enjoy being in a place with punishing noise. They fail to understand the difference between the excitement and festivity of a place filled with the "buzz" of those having a good time and a virtual torture chamber. A busy restaurant or bar can be lively and enjoyable if the acoustics are appropriate, but the same crowd in a place without the proper acoustics is often a horror.

In order for anything to improve further in this area, some more dramatic things have to happen. First of all, the public needs awareness. Second, they have to be made to care about protecting themselves, their children, and others. Third, elected officials need to be pressured into taking action. This is the most difficult obstacle to improvement, because decent public officials should have already been acting on their own. As it is, they have not. They should not have to rely on a grassroots movement to take action on such a serious matter. Unfortunately, they do not profit from efforts in this area. This subject does not have "grandstand" appeal like many other publicized issues. Politicians are quick to appear to be addressing a societal problem like child abuse, but they are ignoring one form of child abuse being unwittingly perpetrated by parents on a regular basis ... and right out in public. That abuse is the exposure of their children to noise! They bring their children to concerts and restaurants and stadiums, but officials do not address this. They ignore it since it will not get them votes and will not get any votes until people perceive the necessity or priority of taking action. Furthermore, special interests will always resist anything that could cost them money or inconvenience. Airports will resist. Factory owners will resist. Local police departments will not want to take on the burden of more laws to enforce. Restaurants will resist. Nightclubs will resist. Concert promoters will resist. Athletic leagues, stadiums, arenas, and competitions will resist. Motorcycle manufacturers will resist. Machine manufacturers will resist. Lawn and landscape services will resist. Sanitation companies will resist. Speaker and audio equipment manufacturers will resist.

It is sad to acknowledge that resistance often translates into political contributions and support for the legislator catering to the special interest while the general public suffers. The public needs to cry out for relief until government representatives have little choice but to act. Little can be done to correct this problem without legislation.

In the matter of controlling noise, it is regrettable that we cannot legislate manners, courtesy, or consideration for others, but if the right pressure is brought to bear, we will be capable of enacting laws to at least require compliance with the standards necessary to improve the health and safety of our citizens.

The reason this chapter is in a book on EP is that it illustrates the use and application of EP in the real world in two ways:

1. Recognition of reality. People are being harmed and sometimes killed by noise every day. This is no less a threat than the dangers on our roadways and exposure to accidents in our homes and places of work.

2. Seeking a pragmatic remedy. The damage from noise intrusion can be minimized and in some case stopped if hard, practical decisions are taken, not just by governments, but also by all of us on a daily basis. This includes homeowners; parents; proprietors of establishments serving the public; and anyone who uses machines, amplifiers, and other equipment. The cause and effect of EP will play out to provide the remedy sought.

Assuming there is an interest in improving our environment and the general health and well-being of our populace regarding this issue, an EPrag might consider recommending the following for achieving the goal:

1. Education of the public as to the real dangers of noise to themselves and their loved ones including teaching about noise in our schools.
2. Enlisting the support of the Surgeon General, the Public Health Service, and other health agencies, including the CDC and NIH, for a campaign similar to that witnessed against the dangers of tobacco.
3. Enlisting the further support of OSHA.
4. Legislation at all levels to minimize noise, such as the following:
   A. Building codes to require insulation against noise in floors, walls, roofs, and ceilings. (All building codes contain standards for structural integrity for good reason, but some requirements, although necessary—like for fire, tornadoes, and hurricanes—are beneficial only sporadically. Noise does harm to everyone every day.)
   B. Decibel caps/ceilings in all places accessed by the public. (The noise problem became so bad at New York City beaches that the then Mayor Ed Koch banned "boom boxes.")
   C. Special legislation as to events such as concerts, sports competitions, rallies, and demonstrations.
   D. Restrictions on the kinds of machines and their emissions of noise, such as generators, compressors, and lawn blowers.
   E. Restrictions on vehicle noise emissions, particularly for motorcycles.
   F. Strict enforcement of all standards.

G. Sensible delegation of enforcement responsibilities with required accountability from all individuals and departments. As an example, boards of health might be charged with policing noise levels in restaurants, while other officials such as in zoning or the actual police departments might monitor shopping malls and events.

You would be correct if you detected some uncharacteristic bias in my writing about noise. In writing this book, it is my declared intention not to take sides in an issue, but I do not believe there is any issue as to noise itself. No one could, in good conscience, credibly contend that excessive noise is good for you. Any controversy in this area would not be reasonably related to the underlying subject, only the decision of whether or not to provide a remedy. There also is no apparent ethical component to this question. It is simply a matter of choice; that is, whether to provide a remedy or not.

As an EPrag, therefore, I would encourage the populace to change some of its habits. As to governments, it remains for the appropriate authorities to decide, but I have offered a possible pragmatic course of action leading to a solution of the problem if one is ever desired.

Chapter 16

Language

Can using EP help us to communicate better?

> Language is the armory of the human mind, and at once
> contains the trophies of its past and the weapons of its future
> conquests.
>
> —Samuel Taylor Coleridge

This chapter is entitled "Language," but for EP purposes it is really about the specific use of language to communicate in contemporary society. For society to function, it is necessary to have a means that enables the delivery of what is in our minds from one person to another. This process can involve the use of words, sounds, signs, or even types of behavior to express or exchange information. As I discuss language here, I am not including artificially constructed communication systems such as codes, cyphers, and computer symbols. I mean to address what is known as natural human language, such as that which is spoken, written, or acted out with hand or body signs.

I mention the specific use of language because there are a number of uses other than simple communication. For example, there is a use for identifying with others, like an ethnic group, or a use in being classified in social stratification (see *Pygmalion*, George Bernard Shaw, and the works of Edward Sapir).

This chapter is discussing language principally as a means of communicating, but even the most basic communication skills and methods may have significance that transcends a simple message. And the importance of language use runs throughout the spectrum of society, from laborers in the field to heads of nations. At higher levels, historian Arthur Schlesinger wrote in his collection of essays *The Cycles of American History* (Houghton Mifflin) that leadership in a democracy is particularly dependent on language:

> Winning consent requires leaders who possess not only a personal vision but also the capacity to communicate that vision to their age ... and the language used by leaders determines the tone of politics. For language is the means by which politics deals with reality. Words may express reality or simplify it or sentimentalize it or reject it.

There are many elements of the uses of language. It can be specific or general, clear or muddled, formal or familiar, and common or sophisticated. It can be changed by tone or context. It can be influenced by gestures. As to language itself, there are an estimated six thousand languages in the world!

Language as a subject for study or simply for categorizing is complex. There are numerous fields of language interest. Just naming these few will indicate how overwhelming it could be to study them:

1. Semantics
2. Semiotics
3. Linguistics
4. Metonymy
5. Synonymy
6. Morphology
7. Ontology
8. Polysemy
9. Phonetics

There are studies of language to determine what it means to *mean* something and studies to determine how we communicate in psycholinguistic and social psychology. Believe it or not, there is even a subcategory of linguistics known as *pragmatics*!

Philosophers have been studying and writing about language throughout the ages, from Plato (400 BC) to Noam Chomsky (1928–). John Stuart Mill said, "Language is the light of the mind." Benjamin Whorf has noted that language shapes the thoughts and emotions determining one's perception of reality. Rousseau believed that language originated from emotions, while Kant said it came from rational and logical thought. There are even those who contend that philosophy itself is in reality the study of language (Ludwig Wittgenstein).

I do not have to tell you how important language is in communicating or how important it is to communicate effectively. Language affects us, and those around us, every day we live. It is the expression of our thoughts—our feelings, needs, hopes, questions, and answers. Language is the quality that makes us human.

Having paid homage to a few of civilization's great names and thinkers, I now say that whether language originated either from emotions (Rousseau) or from rational and logical thought (Kant), it is of absolutely no concern to me in this chapter and to EP in general. It also does not matter what words, terms, or phrases are used to refer to any aspect of language. My concern as an EPrag is to observe what the present condition of language is and, if needed, what can be done to change that condition for the better.

For the purposes of this exercise, English as spoken (or misspoken) in the United States is the only language considered. Based on the observations about language in the United States, it is the author's opinion that we are in serious trouble.

In the development of our country, it took a while for all of the population to have the opportunity to receive even the most basic education. It is understandable that among the immigrant classes and the poor, good speech and writing of any kind were lacking. But the use of English in what was considered to be our educated population was quite good. This deteriorated dramatically after what I believe to be the watershed of our modern culture, the Second World War. Just prior to WWII, for those fortunate enough to have it, formal education for almost all Americans was limited to public elementary and secondary schooling. Even with that, very few completed secondary school. We were struggling through the major economic crisis of the century. Jobs and careers were scarce. In order to compete for the better opportunities in commerce or government, some realized it was necessary to speak and write in a manner that would distinguish oneself. Public schools generally were good. Teaching in the public schools was considered an honorable profession. Teachers were at a level of competence and dedication that commanded respect from pupils, their families, and the community. They capably taught values and skills to those who wanted to learn. As is stated above, many were prevented from learning by family circumstances, living conditions, or societal subjugation. It is not a coincidence that those who did not learn remained at the lowest end of our economy. To me it is a certainty that the kind of language these people knew and used actually prevented them from bettering themselves regardless of their desires and efforts.

The war changed everything. In just a few years, we had moved rapidly from poverty and mass unemployment to a raging economy. At the end of the war, our newly acquired peacetime culture inherited an industrial colossus. The war had over ten million of us in uniform. Out of a population of approximately 140 million, that would amount to the proportional equivalent in 2016 of over 20 million job seekers coming back to the labor force. They needed jobs, housing, and an education. We became the world's supplier of steel and manufactured goods. Much of our position as supplier was assured by the implementation of the Marshall Plan, which allowed us to employ American labor and engage American industry to rebuild Europe. We started a construction and housing boom. We created a new sociological phenomenon—the suburbs. And we ambitiously began educating a wider populace. The GI Bill put people in college that could only have dreamed about higher education before the war. Job forces grew, corporations grew, and schools grew. Then it started to happen.

It did not happen all at once, but insidiously over the next few decades—about one and a half generations. Parents who experienced the war and the Depression didn't want their children to suffer as they had, so they lowered their standards of behavior. We needed more teachers, so we started lowering our standards for teachers. We needed to move more pupils through the system, so we lowered our standards for pupils. Television arrived. Now we could *see* announcers and presenters, so we selected them for looks instead of ability. Basically, what happened following the war was that first we peaked and then we began our decline. This decline is now known as the dumbing down of America.

The decline was not limited to the use of language. Morality, values, behavioral standards as well as educational standards all deteriorated. In this treatment, I am considering only the effects on the use of our language.

Sociologists, psychologists, economists, and political scientists may give you various reasons for the deterioration in the use of our language. It could be the subject of many books, but it is not the subject of this chapter. I am focusing on one small aspect of this to illustrate the use of EP in addressing a situation that needs improvement.

Libraries, bookstores, and websites are filled with information on our language usage. The topics include vocabulary, grammar, rhetoric, syntax, how to speak, how to write, common errors and confused words. There are even games, clubs and organizations about language and much more. There is a lot less about how poor our language usage has become.

I certainly have my pet grievances about misused words and phrases, but for the purposes of this chapter, I am assuming that you, the informed reader, also have some language uses that bother you. I also assume we all agree that we need to get our population communicating more accurately and effectively, whether through speech, in written form, or on electronic social and commercial media. But why should we care about using language correctly? Does it really matter if we use bad grammar? Misuse words? I think it does for at least four reasons:

1. Effective communication minimizes the chances of misunderstandings in social, familial, or business settings.

(Remember the famous story about the comma that cost the government millions of dollars?)

2. Good use of language raises the level of performance of the lowest echelon of our society, making them better workers and citizens.

3. Striving for proper use of language organizes your brain and improves your mind.

4. The ability to recognize poorly used language avoids, among other things, being misled through emotional reactions or through faulty logic.

Regarding the fourth reason above, let us take two iconic American utterances by well-known Americans who presumably meant well in their respective communications. One is Barry Goldwater's "[E]xtremism in the defense of liberty is no vice!" The other is Vince Lombardi's "Winning isn't everything, it's the only thing." Senator Barry Goldwater was expressing his political beliefs, Coach Vince Lombardi his beliefs about athletic competition. I think they were both sincere, but they were also pandering to their respective audiences—Goldwater to those in the political spectrum who supported his views in general and Lombardi to the sporting world's press corps, who relished this type of hyperbole. They also were both wrong.

Extremism in the mind of an EPrag is never justified. Conventional definitions of extremism equate it to radicalism and fanaticism. In our world, these characteristics and the actions relating to them have never led anywhere but to misery. Use of the word in this context produces both a logical fallacy (suggesting that extremism and liberty are equal) and a misleading use, in that it essentially tells the reader that extremism is a virtue.

As for winning, it certainly is not everything, nor is winning *justified* by anything or everything. But, winning or not, neither concept is replaced by indicating that winning is "the only thing." Again, this is a logical fallacy suggesting that winning is so important that it excludes consideration of anyone and anything else in life. This phrase produces nothing more than an emotional reaction not based on reality.

Thus, as is stated in the fourth reason above, learning how to recognize improperly used language can serve as a valuable tool in evaluating the soundness of an utterance. In some situations, a perceptive public capable of recognizing the misuse of language could readily thwart the intentions of evil propagandists.

In terms of using language to improve your mind and thus improve your entire ability to perform in any way, I offer the following thought. We all err in language at one time or another. In this relatively brief discourse on language, or in this book, there may be many errors of various kinds. I have tried to avoid them, but perhaps I did not succeed. This is forgivable. What is not forgivable is not caring at all. Caring about doing something right and doing it as best you can are at the center of many of the world's philosophies, religions, and disciplines, because doing so focuses your mind on a positive goal. This alone can raise your own standards of behavior and self-image.

In order to make the improvements discussed, I put forth an example of how EP might approach this situation.

After having made the proper observations and being sure of the facts about our current condition, as well as evaluating the condition and concluding that action is warranted, we look for a goal. In this case the goal is getting more accurate and correct use of our vocabulary and grammar so that our communication is clear and unambiguous and that *we all talk and write the same way.*

By setting standards for everyone to follow and having everyone strive to meet those standards, we can raise the performance levels and thus the socioeconomic levels of more people.

First, we have to set the standards. In the past our public schools had those standards and taught them. This is no longer the case. In past generations many of us benefited from a number of guiding sources, such as *The Elements of Style* by William Strunk Jr. and E. B White, but this book was first published in 1935. Although later editions are more relevant, the masses today never even heard of Strunk and White, let alone have they read their book.

In order to set the standards, EP suggests the creation of a body to be called something like the "North American (or simply American) Academy of Letters." This should not be a government project at the outset, for fear it will be politicized. Ideally, it should be started by a nonpolitical aggregation of grants with some select universities.

The model for this body could be the Academie Française, which has been setting the standards for French vocabulary, grammar, and literature since 1635. After it establishes its independence and integrity, nonpolitical government funding might be considered. The academy would issue its determinations as to all aspects of language use in the United States in the light of present circumstances. One major goal toward achieving effective, accurate communication, would be to arrive at a working, usable set of standards that would be easy for the entire population to adopt. Following the French model, the academy would seek recognition of all the colleges, universities, public school boards, and governments as the authority on our language. Also, as in the French model and of considerable importance, the academy's findings and standards would only be advisory. Nothing issued or determined by the academy would be binding on anyone—not on the public or on any government.

Some of the areas to address would be those with which the public has great difficulty and that do not always make good sense; for example,

1. Take the nominative/objective case area. In the United States in response to the question "Who's there?" we say, "It's me!" Should this be considered wrong because the objective pronoun "me" is used instead of the nominative "I"? The French addressed this ages ago. In French, to answer in the correct case, one would have to say, "C'est Je," the nominative. This simply doesn't sound right and is difficult to say. Instead, the French use, and the Academie approves, using the objective case, "C'est moi!" This sounds better, is easier to use, and makes more sense. Why should someone be

accused of using bad grammar when he speaks in a way that makes more sense and is more pragmatic?

2. Another nominative/objective case issue involves the words "who" and "whom." "Who did you give it to?" is wrong, but is it really better to be required to say, "To whom did you give it?" How many college-educated people say it that way?

3. We have problems with gender sensitivity, so we are constantly fumbling with "he" and "she" or "his" and "hers." Perhaps we should simply allow "they" and "theirs" as being correct for both plural and singular.

Do not misunderstand what I am saying. As I stated before, correct usage is important, but a review of what is considered correct and what is not has to be made for contemporary reality. There are many misuses that should be pointed out to the general public for correction, including some of the worst offenders, seen and heard on television every day and read in the newspapers constantly. For example, "less people"—ouch! "Don't just lay there!" "They do it like I do." People also have to be taught that "delinquent" is not necessarily related to juveniles or any age group and "chauvinism" has nothing to do with males or pigs. The list is long.

After the standards are set and recognized, we will have created the proverbial level playing field for all to participate in using our language in the same effective manner. Those choosing otherwise cannot then complain about lost opportunities. But there has to be a delivery system that can teach. We do not have it. Teachers themselves have to be held to rigorous performance criteria. To teach, a teacher should be required to score high enough on a test to ensure competency in our language. No language ability, no job.

Next, we need a campaign like the ones to change the smoking habits of the populace some years ago. We have to create an environment where everyone will be eager and proud to be speaking and writing well. We need to enlist the participation of our athletes, movie personalities, and role models of every kind.

In my writings on parenting, I call for more and early education about child development for all of our future parents. The benefit of good language use is a core part of this. The structure of proper language is a valuable tool for young minds. The rules of vocabulary and grammar teach a sense of order and discipline that leads to more effective intellectual growth. I have heard many parents disparage order and discipline in favor of their concept of "creativity." What foolishness! The greatest and most creative artists, composers, and writers of the ages were disciplined and worked with a sense of order in their respective fields. The gift of language skills is the opening of doors for self-esteem and success in every socioeconomic level of our population.

Chapter 17

Leadership

I am not afraid of an army of lions led by a sheep; I am afraid of an army of sheep led by a lion.

—Alexander the Great

Vision is the art of seeing what is invisible to others.

—Jonathan Swift

The pessimist complains about the wind; the optimist expects it to change; the realist adjusts the sails.

—William Arthur Ward

Do not go where the path may lead, go instead where there is no path and leave a trail.

—Ralph Waldo Emerson

In the animal kingdom, of which our ancestors were once a part, there have been leaders and followers since the time that animals, as we now know them, first came into existence. Today we observe this on the plains of Africa, in the jungles of South America—on all continents—as well as in and around our mountains, rivers, and oceans. Even insects function under some sort of hierarchy, notably bees and ants with their highly structured societies. So has it always been with man, whether tribal chieftains, medicine men, clerics, kings, generals and other military officers, emperors, presidents, owners, chairmen, or heads of a household.

Exactly what it is that constitutes a leader is rather complex and often relates to the values of a particular culture or the set of circumstances in a given time. In the earliest stage of human existence, the leader was principally the strongest man or best fighter. Occasionally, it was someone who was thought to have supernatural powers or some sacral presence connecting him with primitive deities or natural phenomena. Sometimes in more advanced civilizations it was one who was deemed to possess the wisdom necessary to guide his people to survival in the face of adversity. Often it was a combination of things, as in the case of the Sumerian princes over four thousand years ago, who were considered figuratively to be "shepherds" over a population consisting metaphorically of sheep. It was officially acknowledged even then that the few were destined to lead the many. In the case of the princes, a responsibility was also assumed, because during their reign it was implied that they would provide sustenance and protection to their flock. Whatever it was that constituted leaders, initially they all had one common trait—superiority in one form or another.

As the world evolved, other factors began to influence how leaders came into power or were selected. Heredity started playing a role long ago, with various justifications. One such justification was the belief that the right of an ancestor to rule originally resulted from some divine occurrence and thus could be passed on to progeny. There were more practical reasons, principally of a political nature, like protection of wealth, consolidation of power, or fear of incursion. And then there were out-and-out conquests—showing that certain human traits had not changed much since the beginning of the human experience.

For millennia practices based on succession or conquest were the norm, until we came to the era when the populace became empowered, usually by what has become the conventional way of choosing leaders—the vote.

Once the public became involved, it was inevitable that political groups or parties, in one form or another, would come into existence so that the influence of individuals could be aggregated. Those favoring either a particular leader or a system of beliefs joined together to oppose those who favored a different leader or belief system. So it is today in most of the world in government and in institutions and organizations of every conceivable type. But how then are the leaders constituted? The following is one sad perspective and a great incentive to utilize the principles of EP.

If you believe that there is a lack of quality leadership around the world, you will appreciate these thoughts and observations. First, let us consider four areas where the nature and quality of leadership, wherever it is exercised, can impact the lives of all of us around the globe:

1. The private sector/commerce/nonprofit organizations, etc.
2. The military
3. Religion
4. Government and the public sector

Let us look at the commercial part of the first area listed above. If functioning in a free enterprise system, the principal motivation for almost all actions is profit. In this realm, leaders traditionally had been chosen for their real, rather than perceived, ability to perform. Historically, good leaders rose to the top because they were innovative, creative, hardworking, and competent administrators. Commencing prior to the Industrial Revolution but accelerating rapidly in the middle of the nineteenth century, the leaders who emerged or were chosen appear to have delivered at the least what was anticipated and normally very much more. This phenomenon did much to catapult the United States into the great world industrial power it became. The momentum of success carried this superior leadership tradition well into the twentieth century and spread into parts of the community not necessarily concerned purely with profit, such as foundations, charities, and public service organizations. Unfortunately, this tradition of superiority began to wear out around the edges as a result of questionable practices, which will be addressed further on.

As to area two, military leaders in some parts of the world ascend to a position of great power by the illicit exercise of force in a criminal, violent manner or as a concomitant of some political revolutionary thrust or internal treachery. In other places, generally those with democratic principles, military leaders progress up a hierarchical ladder according to a set of generally accepted rules, laws, and practices.

Regarding area three, various religions provide the methods of choosing leaders in a huge assortment of ways. Some believe potential leaders are born to lead and are sought out and identified in their years of infancy. Others rely on scholarship and an avowed commitment to faith to qualify for a leadership position, and still others use a system akin to the political activities practiced in a secular environment.

Area four, government, is the most dramatic area to examine because when one considers all the incompetency and corruption of leadership throughout the world, this area stands out far above all others. So I am choosing to use the area of government as an example. We should begin by pointing out some of the causes that result in the declining ability of our leaders to lead effectively.

Let us invoke one of the precepts of EP for a preliminary analysis— recognition of reality. In government, the problems begin at the polls. Yes, the empowered populace that initially brought us those marvelous ideals embodied in democratic values has now degenerated to such an extent as to be the principal culprit in the long-term drought of good leaders. It is true that other factors, such as the lure of industry, academia, or other endeavors, deprive government of many potential leaders, but ultimately a choice has to be made from what is available.

EP cannot quickly change world practices and habits that have developed insidiously over the last two centuries, but it can stimulate an awareness that might modify individual, if not group, perspectives regarding the selection of leaders by voting. If only one of EP's principles were followed, great progress could be forthcoming almost immediately. This one principle is the recognition of reality.

In virtually every country in the world where there are free elections, the principal characteristics sought by the electorate seem to be good looks, charm, and personality, three things that have very little, if anything at all, to do with someone's ability to govern or act as a representative of others. Those qualities may be highly beneficial in choosing an entertainer, a public relations spokesperson, or a prom queen, but not a chief of state or member of a representative assembly.

Every four years in the United States we have a presidential election. We are challenged to consider filling the most powerful office in the world—politically, industrially, and militarily. This individual is to be commander-in-chief of the military and head of the executive branch of the world's most powerful government. How do Americans meet this challenge? Sadly, Americans vote as if they were choosing their high school senior class president. This is insane!

The practice of electing officials in this foolhardy manner does not simply apply to the president of the United States. It applies to elections for all offices in America—local and national—whether for an executive office; a legislative assembly; a board, panel, or council of any kind; and, regrettably, for the judiciary as well. This harmful phenomenon unfortunately prevails to some degree in almost every country where free elections are held, and it is blessed, fostered, and promoted by the press. Why does the press do this? Because of the prevailing motivations and goals of most of the press, principally improving readership and viewership. The overall influence of the press is better (and more nefariously) served by covering, publicizing, and addressing the activities of the more glamorous candidates, regardless of their abilities, over those who are more capable, serious, and less flamboyant. Charisma beats quality every time.

How can the principles of EP be applied to improve this situation? With a public awareness campaign emphasizing reality by ignoring labels and superficial characteristics and an analysis and evaluation based solely upon cause and effect without regard to corrupting influences. In this context, corrupting influences are principally the emotions that cause us to respond more favorably to a smile, manner of speech, or ability to engage in social activities with which we identify than to competency. Doing this involves the essentials of critical thinking—the same kind of critical thinking described in chapter 7 of this book and the application of common sense as indicated in chapter 6. In evaluating a candidate for any office, those less articulate, less handsome/pretty, and less "hip" who have demonstrated greater integrity, competency, compassion, and intelligence need to be given the appropriate respect, consideration, and support.

One further thought relating to government—in modern times, and particularly in a multicultural society, effective leadership cannot be accomplished by ideologues. Leaders must be pragmatists.

These recommendations apply to other areas where leaders are chosen, such as in the corporate world. After the commencement of practices like affirmative action and political correctness, both endorsed and exploited by the press for their own gains (the conflicts, divisiveness, etc., arising from these practices make good stories), the corporate world abandoned the standards by which leaders formerly rose to the summit of corporate leadership. The result was a cascade of mediocrity. This has prevailed somewhat in labor unions, in the administration of education, and in most of the institutions that made America great. This ubiquitous decline may, in fact, be responsible for America's beginning to slip as the world's biggest economy, in the loss of its previously colossal manufacturing infrastructure, in the exportation of jobs, and in the frequent weakening of the dollar, because without leaders who have vision and the ability to manage, innovate, and perform effectively, all aspects of life suffer.

The foregoing are just a few thoughts about the application of EP principles in some areas, but the same principles apply to all situations in which leadership is a concern. Whether in military, religious, private, commercial, public service, fraternal, or governmental realms, or any other setting in the human experience where leadership is a factor, EP principles apply.

Chapter 18

Can Ethical Pragmatism
Save The World?

I know not with what weapons World War III will be fought,
but World War IV will be fought with sticks and stones.

—Albert Einstein

You ask, what is our aim? I can answer in one word. It is victory,
victory at all costs, victory in spite of all terror, victory, however
long and hard the road may be; for without victory, there is no
survival.

—Winston S. Churchill

The title of this chapter sounds like a bit of a joke. The question cannot be serious, you think, because it sounds a bit dramatic, if not megalomaniacal, for a writer to dare pose something so ambitious. Well, here it is anyway.

To even consider answering this absurd question, you must assume that the world is doomed. You next have to examine why the world is doomed and then determine what pragmatic steps need to be taken to change the course of the world's presumed destiny.

All right, as you may have guessed, this is just another exercise to demonstrate what might be done through the application of EP if it were necessary to save the world. And for this exercise you have to assume "the world" is man's world; that is, a world inhabited and dominated by man, because even if man ceased to be on Earth, it is fairly certain there would still be a world—the planet Earth—in the Sun's (solar) planetary system. Let us consider a not-so-far-fetched scenario.

First of all, Earth is not the planet of humans. Man has not been on Earth long enough to have earned that honor. Throughout known history, if any life form other than amoeba-like creatures could be given the title associated with Earth, it would probably be the dinosaurs. They dominated the Earth for about 180 million years. I am usually amazed by how many people have no conception of this. Just think of fossil fuels alone. Much of the oil we dig up, drill for, and have been using in the millions of barrels daily for over a century is from the remains of dinosaurs! Even before dinosaurs, fossils from other creatures and flora were establishing this huge mass in our earth. On top of all that, the dinosaur carcasses piled up and sank into the ground over the millions and millions of years when they roamed the Earth and then got geologically compressed. All those things formed what we extract as crude oil. The dinosaurs lost their ownership of what we now think of as our world only through natural phenomena, probably asteroid strikes millions of years ago.

Following the disappearance of the dinosaurs, we had to wait about sixty-five million more years until man arrived. We cannot tell exactly when we humans became humans on this planet, but in terms of the planet's existence, it is barely a wink in a lifetime—perhaps forty thousand years ago if we are generous to ourselves. By time comparison, it is like we really just got here. To think we have always been here and will always be is what might reasonably be considered naïveté in the extreme.

Since those early days of man until now, the existence of man on Earth has been threatened only by occasional potential natural disasters, like asteroids, floods, and biological events such as plagues. Notwithstanding speculation and fantasies like those of Nostradamus and some hysterics, man's own acts thus far have not threatened to completely extinguish our species on this planet. One very good reason man has not threatened to end his own reign is that he has not had the power to do it. Another reason was that there was not a significant presence, if any at all, of those whose aim was to destroy the entire world. So it is not just a question of technology, weapons of mass destruction, nuclear bombs, and biological or chemical warfare. It is also a question of the conduct of the world's population— particularly extremists. The prevailing human mentality of the past did not countenance destroying our entire world. We have a different situation in the modern era.

Many things could be done by following EP that might contribute toward saving the world. Among them are effective research about diseases and infirmities, development of better technologies to help feed our population, and pragmatic actions regarding the environment. However, this chapter will focus on what I consider to be the most immediate area of concern. This area is a part of the phenomenon that I believe to be man's greatest failure—war! When I mention war, I mean armed conflict in all its forms, not just the traditional concept of large groups facing each other on the field of battle. It includes that part of the phenomenon, as you will read here, in which the world can be destroyed by unilateral action alone.

Until relatively recently, like the last thousand years, and, in most cases, a lot less, the human population of our world was small and the masses were not empowered. The skills and weapons necessary for personal and group combat were reserved for the nobility and the few of a select, elite class. The small general population had no knowledge about warfare or the ability to wage war. Even the battles of antiquity, the Roman conquests, the Crusades, and the exploits of Genghis Kahn, which produced the world's greatest empire with an army of two hundred thousand, involved but a minute portion of the population. Even at that, their armies and those of the likes of Alexander and Hannibal consisted principally of warriors who were sociologically akin to sheep. They followed the orders of their respective leaders and depended on their leaders for their very existence. They had no independent way of functioning.

There are great differences between the war machines of yesteryear and those of today. Look at the conquerors of the past. They are usually one person—Alexander the Great, Hannibal, Caesar, Suleiman the Magnificent, and Napoleon. These figures were often usurpers in one form or another who were able to rise above an ignorant, unskilled, and backward populace to be demigods and conduct their campaigns against usually easily subjugated peoples and regions. Yes, there were secular authorities of sorts, as with the Greek states, the Romans, and historical monarchies like that of Richard I, but the power used by these figures was never derived from the illiterate, unenlightened, and powerless masses.

Through the ages, the world population increased. More and more people came in contact with one another and began exchanging goods, services, and eventually thoughts and ideas. Elements of the population became literate. Abilities to travel and communicate evolved. The American Revolution shocked the world, and the granite feet of the aristocracy began changing into clay. In the nineteenth century the Industrial Revolution took hold like a juggernaut—railroads, steamships, telegraphy, inventions, mass production, the growth of cities, labor movements, revolutions, and wars. Ultimately, the masses were empowered. They could read and write. They had a voice in the press. They could demonstrate. They could strike. They could vote. They could participate in the process of the authority that controlled their destiny.

As has been pointed out, one major result of this questionable progress and popular empowerment was war. It was war on a grand scale, a scale bigger and more deadly than ever could have been contemplated in the primitive times of the past. We "progressed" into wars that were so horrific in scope that two of them in the twentieth century were called world wars. The masses were now in it. They became nationalistic. They participated in the governments that waged war. They invented, improved, manufactured, and used the tools of a modern war—tools for more killing, more maiming, more destruction, and more misery.

Now we are at an age when many technologies have matured to a level that makes them readily available to everyone. We have electronic communications of every variety, like cellular telephones, instant messaging, and social media. We have Internet access that allows us to search for, locate, and obtain every kind of damaging device and substance. We have the capability to electronically spy on, and steal from, legitimate military networks. Very little technology is unavailable to those wishing to do harm.

As to practical ability to apply the technology, the masses now have the means to act upon and sustain their ambitions. Global financial resources are now available to support dangerous movements and evil terrorist ideologies. Some terror groups have access to their own funding, such as revenue from the oil fields around the world. Rogue nations have the enormous resources of an entire country at their disposal.

It may be that it was the social and political development of the masses that facilitated the evolution of the technologies of war. Unfortunately, that same development additionally provided a much wider political and economic support base for the launching of fanatically driven agendas.

The rise of the Nazi Party after World War I, culminating in Adolph Hitler's ascent to dictator, was fueled by industrialists and support from the citizenry. The enormity of Hitler's monstrosity—the death toll alone—challenges the imagination. But he actually wanted it to be even worse. In 1945, when it became obvious that Germany's Third Reich would have to surrender unconditionally to the Allied forces, Hitler, now recognized as a fanatical, insane, drug-dependent mass murderer, issued orders to destroy Germany—all of Germany! He meant to have the entire country reduced to ruins and everyone in his own country dead. By then his only remaining control was over Germany and, although being close to developing one, he did not have a nuclear bomb. Some of his orders were carried out by Nazi zealots, but most ignored the orders because of the proximity of the liberating forces and the fear of postwar repercussions. Today, another fanatic issuing the same orders might succeed. All that is needed is a sufficient number of nuclear warheads, chemical or biological weapons, or a combination of all of these released with fervor on the entire world, and that could do it.

Remember, EP is not a faith. Adherence to it is a matter of choice; in fact, following the principles of EP requires that before you decide to follow them, *you first have to follow them in order to decide to follow them.* You have to observe and analyze the tenets of EP in the light of reality, evaluate them objectively, and conclude that by applying the standards in any given situation you will attain the intended goal. After having drawn that conclusion, you are ready to address any and all questions, situations, propositions, conflicts, problems, or issues.

In addressing any issue, like the survival of the world, EP demands that all observations recognize reality. The prospect of world destruction through any or a combination of all of the threats—Cyber-Armageddon, nuclear conflagration, catastrophic pollution, and super-pandemic—is real. It is scientifically demonstrable. Terrorist extremists with the capability of using these instrumentalities are a reality.

Having recognized the reality and then made the necessary analysis and evaluation, one only has to decide on a course of action. Platitudes, euphemisms, and political and social ideologies will not do it. No military or terrorist act was ever stopped by conversation. After my chapter on religion, I included an old article I wrote about the ancient Thugs in India. The history I related may well be a microcosmic portrayal of our current circumstances. The lesson of that history is enduring:

The only pragmatic approach to a challenge like this is to do *all* that is necessary to completely eliminate it at its roots and for all time. This requires making the most difficult decisions to engage in a campaign of very distasteful acts, regardless of opposition from groups, factions, governments, and individuals with their respective agendas and outlooks. Would that we acquire the leadership necessary to accomplish this goal.

Conclusion

Ethical pragmatism offers hope to all those who grapple with daily challenges, ranging from the most mundane to those of life-altering significance for ourselves alone or for the entire world population. It is a philosophy to be used by us, as individuals in our personal lives. It is a philosophy to be used by those in government, industry, science, the arts and in every endeavor, organization and institution in the human experience. Whatever decision is made, whatever action is contemplated— all will be aided by adopting a few simple standards and governing your behavior by doing the following:

1. Making use of your brain and becoming a critical thinker.
2. Systematically observing, analyzing, evaluating, and concluding.
3. Disregarding all corrupting influences by resisting your emotions.
4. Ignoring labels and the intimidation of others regarding the subject under consideration.
5. Objectively identifying your goal.
6. Avoiding self-deception.
7. Realistically and unemotionally determining what action will produce your intended goal.
8. Applying common sense to all of the above and to everything you ever do.

In a final parting word, I urge you to start using EP principles and ultimately aspire to being an EPrag. Why do I think this will help you to a better life? Well, for the answer, just use your common sense!

Excerpts of the Author's Words, Phrases, and Thoughts

(Some of the following words or phrases have been coined by the author, some phrases are original usages, and others may have been used before in other applications. The thoughts are original characterizations.)

Words and Phrases

Auditory aesthetics (ch. 15)
Auditory ambiance pollution (ch. 15)
Cogito ergo cogito (ch. 1)
Competitive politics (Introduction)
Corrupting emotions (Preface)
Disingenuous euphemism (ch. 4)
Distribution of assets (ch. 9)
EPrag (Introduction)
Gratuitous amplified percussion, or GAP (ch. 15)
Illusory pragmatism (ch. 8)
Inadvertent pragmatism (ch. 2)
Modified relativism (ch. 1)
Noise intrusion (ch. 15)
Quasi-science (ch. 5)
Shadow-science (ch. 5)
Simple is not simplistic (ch. 3)
Tempered objectivity (ch. 1)

Transfer of assets (ch. 9)
Trial and result (ch. 1)
Ugo = ultimate goal (ch. 7)

Thoughts

"[T]here is no more important part of humanity than you." (Preface)

"A philosophy must do more than attempt to explain. It must do something other than being a topic for a classroom discussion." (Introduction)

"Compassion is the mother of kindness, and there can never be too much kindness in any human endeavor." (ch. 1)

"Pragmatism, in and of itself, can go nowhere but to ruin." (ch. 2)

"Wisdom is a cultural compound consisting of experience and common sense." (ch. 3)

"The value of human life is the underlying basis of universal morality." (ch. 4)

"Humans have the ability to change what nature has prescribed." (ch. 4)

"[W]e should never compromise principles, but always be willing to compromise positions." (ch. 4)

"The credo of ethical pragmatism is to seek, by thought and reason through rational behavior and action, the best method of achieving the most desirable goals of mankind for the greatest number of people." (ch. 4)

"There is no indication of there being a dispute between the left and the right when the wheel was being invented!" (ch. 4)

"No one should ever be labeled for expressing an opinion." (ch. 4)

"Ethical pragmatism is not an absolute, rigid philosophy but a living, tolerant, evolving way of dealing with all human challenges, endeavors, and issues." (ch. 4)

"Wisdom is the compound produced by merging experience *with* common sense." (ch. 6)

"[W]e are human beings. This means that we should not be behaving like sheep." (ch. 7)

"Be honest with yourself. This realization of the truth may be uncomfortable, but it is necessary." (End of Part One)

"Not having the accurate facts before acting is tantamount to erecting a skyscraper on quicksand." (Introduction to Part 2)

"God created man so that man could create justice." (ch. 10 and 11)

"[J]ustice is a concept that was created by man in his earliest stages of becoming part of a civilization." (ch. 11)

"Perceived injustice is the motivator of much societal activity and a major contributor to violence." (ch. 11)

"[U]nless man achieves justice, it does not occur." (ch. 11)

"[A] government's actions in appointing a staff of taxpayer-compensated lawyers to defend a career criminal in a capital case will not impress a citizen who is wrongfully required to pay a parking fine." (ch. 11 Notes)

"The underlying and fundamental motivator, of which economics is the progeny, is basic human insecurity or, or more accurately, the instinct to survive." (ch. 11 Notes)

"Language affects us, and those around us, every day we live. It is the expression of our thoughts—our feelings, needs, hopes, questions, and answers. Language is the quality that makes us human." (ch. 16)

"The greatest and most creative artists, composers, and writers of the ages were disciplined and worked with a sense of order in their respective fields." (ch. 16)

"[T]he principal characteristics sought by the electorate seem to be good looks, charm, and personality, three things that have very little, if anything at all, to do with someone's ability to govern or act as a representative of others." (ch. 17)

"Americans vote as if they were choosing their high school senior class president." (ch. 17)

"[I]n modern times, and particularly in a multicultural society, effective leadership cannot be accomplished by ideologues. Leaders must be pragmatists." (ch. 17)

"The prevailing human mentality of the past did not countenance destroying our entire world. We have a different situation in the modern era." (ch. 18)

Glossary of Proper Names

Aesop (620 – 564 BCE) Ancient Greek teller of stories known for his eponymous fables, many of which are characterized by personification of animals or inanimate objects.

Alexander the Great, aka Alexander III (356–323). Macedonian king who during his brief seven-year reign established himself as one of the greatest generals and military heroes in history.

Aquinas, Thomas (1225–74). Italian Roman Catholic priest of the Dominican Order, teacher, theologian, jurist, and philosopher, and proponent of scholasticism. His enormous contributions in the areas of ethics, natural law, metaphysics, and political theory and lifelong work resulted in his being canonized in 1323.

Aristotle (384–322 BCE). Thinker, logician, scientist, and one of the three famous philosophers of ancient Greece who provided the foundation for future thought in all of Western civilization.

Beard, Charles (1874–1948). Prolific American historian advancing various theories, including his most famous relating to the position that the motivations for drafting the US Constitution were principally economic.

Beattie, James (1735–1803). Scottish poet, writer, and philosophy professor whose works influenced Robert Burns, Sir Walter Scott, and Lord Byron.

Buddha (563–483 BCE). Title given to Siddhartha Gautama, Nepalese philosopher, teacher, and religious thinker whose values and beliefs provide the foundation of the great religion of Buddhism.

Caesar, Julius (100 BCE–44 CE). Patrician figure of ancient Rome and one of the greatest generals in history. Politician, statesman, writer, conqueror, dictator.

Charlemagne (742–814). King of the Franks and consolidator of what became the Holy Roman Empire, of which he was emperor.

Chomsky, Noam (1928–). Acclaimed grammarian, writer, linguist, and political activist responsible for revolutionizing the study of language analysis and linguistics.

Churchill, Winston S. (1874–1965). Great statesman, author, and orator; prime minister of England. Considered by many to be the most important figure of the twentieth century.

Cicero, Marcus Tullius (106 BCE–43 BCE). One of the outstanding figures of ancient Rome. Orator, statesman, scholar, lawyer, and patriot.

Coleridge, Samuel Taylor (1772–1834). English poet, author, and literary theorist of the English Romantic period.

Confucius (551–479 BCE). Chinese philosopher, teacher, and political theorist whose ideas, beliefs, and aphorisms continue to influence cultures around the world.

Critchley, Simon (1960–). English philosopher and author known for works regarding the history of philosophy, religion, ethics, political theory, literature, and theater.

Dalai Lama (1935–). Title of the leader of Tibetan Buddhists given currently to Tenzin Gyatso (fourteenth Dalai Lama). The position is filled by divine guidance to one who then dispenses wisdom and interpretations of Buddhist theory.

Davison, Emily (1872–1913). British suffragette who is celebrated for her actions at the Epsom Derby on June 4, 1913, when, in an act of protest, she stepped in front of King George V's horse during the race, suffering fatal injuries.

Descartes, Rene (1596–1650). French philosopher and mathematician credited with being the father of modern philosophy.

Dewey, John (1859–1952). American psychologist, educator, and philosopher who made major contributions to the field of pragmatism.

Einstein, Albert (1879–1955). German-born physicist and Nobel laureate who continued his astounding career in the United States. Recognized as a genius and one of the world's most creative thinkers of all time, he is most associated with his theory of relativity.

Elizabeth I (1533–1603). Queen of England and daughter of Henry VIII. Recognized as one of the greatest monarchs in history.

Emerson, Ralph Waldo (1803–82). American essayist, poet, lecturer, and exponent of New England transcendentalism, supporting notions of intellectual reason and individual thought.

Gandhi, Mohandas (1869–1948). Given the title "Mahatma" (Great Soul) for his dedication to human rights in the Indian subcontinent and the independence movement in India through nonviolent civil disobedience.

Genghis Kahn (1162–1227). Great Mongolian conqueror who consolidated regional tribes into a unified force that he governed and which produced an astounding empire extending from China to the Adriatic Sea.

Goethe, Johann Wolfgang von (1749–1832). German literary giant with enormous talent, capable of achievements as a critic, journalist, novelist, educational theorist, playwright, poet, scientist, and philosopher.

Goldwater, Barry (1909–98). United States senator and presidential candidate widely supported for his views on political conservatism.

Greeley, Horace (1811–72). American newspaper editor, reformer, abolitionist, and unsuccessful political candidate for the American presidency in 1872.

Gutenberg, Johannes (ca. 1395–1468). German craftsman and inventor who changed the world by originating a method of printing from movable type (now referred to as the printing press).

Hale, Edward Everett (1822–1909). American clergyman, journalist, and author ("The Man Without a Country").

Hannibal (247–182 BCE). Famed general of Asia Minor who led the Carthaginian armies against Rome and whose career was noted for spectacular military exploits in the ancient world.

Hegel, Georg (1770–1831). Great German thinker and philosopher whose brilliant theses contributed significantly to the development of idealism, existentialism, and Marxism.

Hitchens, Christopher (1949–2011). English-born journalist who had an extensive career in the United States as an author, lecturer, media personality, and literary critic.

Howard, Phillip K. (1948–). American lawyer and popular writer in the fields of government and societal reform.

Hume, David (1711–76). Scottish historian, economist, essayist, and philosopher known for his work in the field of empiricism.

Huxley, Thomas (1825–95). British scientist who achieved world fame for his work about Darwinism, educational reform, and methods of teaching science.

Ingersoll, Robert Green (1833–99) Nineteenth-century American lawyer, politician, orator, and popular lecturer known as "the great agnostic."

James, William (1843–1910). American psychologist, writer, and philosopher; brother of novelist Henry James; led the philosophical movement of pragmatism, which sparked a renewed interest in American philosophical study.

Kant, Immanuel (1724–1804). East Prussian–born thinker and great philosopher whose enlightened works influenced virtually all subsequent philosophical study.

Kendall, George (ca.1570–1608). Soldier and captain in the Jamestown Colony of Virginia, where he also served as a member of the Jamestown Council. He is reputed to have been the first person to be executed in the colonies.

Kierkegaard, Soren (1813–55). Danish theologian and philosopher; critic of rationalism; regarded as the founder of existentialism.

King, Martin Luther, Jr. (1929–1968). American clergyman and leader of the civil rights movement in the United States in the postwar period. Winner of the Nobel Peace Prize in 1964.

Koch, Edward Irving ("Ed") (1924–2013). American lawyer, politician, commentator, and media personality who was the 105th mayor of New York City from 1978 through 1989.

Lauder, Estee (1908–2004). Highly successful American entrepreneur whose eponymous cosmetics company was an industry leader for generations.

Lazarus, Emma (1849–87). Nineteenth-century American writer and poet whose famous sonnet "The New Colossus" appears on the Statue of Liberty in New York Harbor.

Leo III, Pope and Saint (d/b unknown–816). Cleric at the time of the struggle between Byzantium and the West who is noted for his actions relating to the emperor Charlemagne.

Lincoln, Abraham (1809–65). Sixteenth president of the United States.

Lombardi, Vince (1913–70). American sports figure who attained national fame as the popular and highly successful football coach of the Green Bay (Wisconsin) Packers.

Mill, John Stuart (1806–73). English economist, politician, and utilitarian philosopher who espoused the rights of the individual and had profound influence on the entire world.

Napoleon (Bonaparte) (1769–1821). Great general and emperor of France, extending his dominion over much of Europe and leaving an indelible mark on Western civilization.

Nietzsche, Friedrich (1844–1900). German philosopher and scholar whose influence on Western philosophy has endured until the present.

Nostradamus aka Michel de Notredame or Nostradame (1503–66). French physician and astrologer known principally for his controversial prophesies.

Paine, Thomas (1737–1809). Political journalist and pamphleteer known for his influence on garnering support for the American Revolution, particularly through his work *Common Sense.*

Pankhurst, Emmeline (1858–1928). Champion of women's suffrage in Great Britain.

Peirce, Charles Sanders (1839–1914). Philosopher, scientist, and logician known for his works about pragmatism as a method of research.

Plato (428–348 BCE). Ancient Greek philosopher who laid the intellectual groundwork for Western culture.

Rand, Ayn (1905–82). Russian-born American writer and novelist of great success who developed the philosophy know as objectivism.

Richard I (1157–99). English king known as Richard the Lionheart who spent most of his reign fighting in foreign wars such as the Crusades.

Roosevelt, Theodore (1858–1919). Twenty-sixth president of the United States. Writer, soldier, and explorer who expanded the powers of the American presidency and federal government.

Rousseau, Jean-Jacques (1712–78). French writer, political theorist, and philosopher whose works were inspirational to the leaders of the French Revolution.

Rustin, Bayard (1912–87). American leader in movements for civil rights, socialism, nonviolence, and gay rights who had considerable influence over the beliefs of Martin Luther King Jr.

Sagan, Carl (1934–1996). American scientist and astronomer whose works are significant in the area of research about extraterrestrial life and early life on Earth.

Saint-Exupéry, Antoine de (1900–44). French writer, war hero, and aviator.

Salk, Jonas (1914–95). American scientist and medical researcher who, as a virologist, discovered and developed the first vaccine for the prevention of paralytic poliomyelitis (infantile paralysis/polio).

Sapir, Edward (1884–1939). Polish-born American anthropologist and linguist and founder of the field of ethnolinguistics.

Sarton, Mary (1912–95). Belgian-born American poet and novelist.

Schlesinger, Arthur (1888–1965). Noted American writer and historian who produced numerous insightful works about various periods and events in history.

Shakespeare, William (1564–1616). Poet, playwright, and dramatist considered to be the greatest writer of all time.

Shaw, George Bernard (1856–1950). Irish-born British playwright of renown whose plays often evoke themes of social reform.

Socrates (470–399 BCE). Along with Plato and Aristotle, one of the three great philosophers of ancient Greece, who ironically seems to have written nothing but is immortalized in the works of others.

Solomon (lived ca. 10th century BCE). Son of and successor to King David of Judea; King Solomon is famed for his poetry, wisdom, and military prowess, all of which are described in the Old Testament.

Spinoza, Baruch aka Benedict de Spinoza (1632–77). Born in Holland to a Portuguese family, Spinoza was a religious thinker and philosopher who is credited with formulating a revolutionary metaphysical system profoundly affecting Western philosophy.

Suleiman (or Suleyman) the Magnificent (1494–1566). Sultan of the mid-sixteenth-century Ottoman Empire who is lauded for his military deeds and achievements in literature, art, architecture, and law.

Swift, Jonathan (1667–1745). Anglo-Irish poet, writer, churchman, and political critic regarded by many as the greatest satirist in the English language.

Thales of Miletus (lived ca. 580 BCE). Ancient Greek figure who left no writings but has been described in various works as a great thinker and statesman who may have been the first philosopher as we know the concept today.

Thoreau, Henry David (1817–62). American poet, author, naturalist, historian, philosopher, and early proponent of the concept of civil disobedience.

Truman, Harry (1884–1972). Thirty-third president of the United States who served at the close of World War II and whose administration instituted the Marshall Plan (1948) and NATO (1949).

Voltaire (François-Marie Arouet, 1694–1778). French satirist, poet, novelist, writer, historian, and philosopher of the Period of Enlightenment whose works espoused human rights and frequently directed harsh criticism at the Catholic Church.

Ward, William Arthur (1921–94). American poet and prolific writer famed for inspirational aphorisms.

Whorf, Benjamin (1897–1941). Follower of Edward Sapir (see this Glossary), but nonetheless a force in the field of linguistics relating language to culture; one such piece of work is known as the Whorfian Hypothesis.

Wittgenstein, Ludwig (1889–1951). Austro-British philosopher acknowledged as an innovator in philosophical thought for his theories on logic and language.

Index

www.ingramcontent.com/pod-product-compliance
Lightning Source LLC
Chambersburg PA
CBHW030438290526
45786CB00001B/339